T0383145

Lean Today, Rich Tomorrow

Succeeding in Today's Globalization Chaos

Joe Bichai

Lean Today, Rich Tomorrow

Succeeding in Today's Globalization Chaos

CRC Press
Taylor & Francis Group
Boca Raton   London   New York

CRC Press is an imprint of the
Taylor & Francis Group, an **informa** business

A PRODUCTIVITY PRESS BOOK

CRC Press
Taylor & Francis Group
6000 Broken Sound Parkway NW, Suite 300
Boca Raton, FL 33487-2742

Printed on acid-free paper
Version Date: 20140805

International Standard Book Number-13: 978-1-4822-3564-7 (Hardback)

Library of Congress Cataloging-in-Publication Data

Bichai, Joe, 1956-
    Lean today, rich tomorrow : succeeding in today's globalization chaos / Joe Bichai.
        pages cm
    Includes bibliographical references and index.
    ISBN 978-1-4822-3564-7 (hardcover : alk. paper) 1. Lean manufacturing. 2. Just-in-time systems. 3. Industrial management. I. Title.

TS155.B486 2015
658--dc23   2014027995

Visit the Taylor & Francis Web site at
http://www.taylorandfrancis.com

and the CRC Press Web site at
http://www.crcpress.com

To my parents, Olga and Jean,

who taught me their sense of professionalism and
passed on their values of honesty, perseverance, and pride.

To Monique Castonguay,

a tireless, devoted worker with great integrity,
without whom this project would never have succeeded.

Contents

Preface

The idea for writing a book came to me when I was traveling home from China in 1998. I had a 15-hour flight ahead of me and, because I can't sleep on planes, I had to find something interesting to do. I'm in the habit of bringing a new book with me every time I travel. These books are always on the same subject range, the things I'm passionate about: just in time (JIT)* and the Lean* Toyota Production System (TPS)*. But I have to say that after reading a dozen such books, I didn't have much left to learn. And one thing stood out in all of them: they described theoretical concepts where everything is nice, simple, and easy to implement. However, my experience had been very different. Our company, Genfoot, was already in its fifth year of Lean/TPS implementation, and we still had a number of problems to fix. Unfortunately, none of the books I'd read told us how to solve them. It seemed to me that it was high time someone wrote about the kinds of problems that any business hoping to implement the Lean/TPS system must face. And I had the sense that I was well placed to do this because our company was a pioneer in this production philosophy within the shoe industry, and we'd had to tackle a number of gigantic obstacles. However, I could honestly say that even if small problems still persisted 20 years later, our work had succeeded. As well, my recent trips to Taiwan and Japan had given me the opportunity to move ahead quickly with my writing project.

I must admit, however, that I had a few reservations about writing this book. First, I wasn't sure how much interest it would attract from readers, particularly managers, professors, and students in engineering or operations management. Second, I didn't want to reveal all our little secrets to our competitors, even if there weren't many of them left in North America!

I changed my mind about that after my visit to the Toyota plant in Japan. I was surprised to meet a delegation of Volvo directors there. As far as I know, the two manufacturers are certainly competitors! But when I questioned a Toyota director about it, he replied that he saw no problem because the factory is in constant transformation. What we see today won't be there tomorrow... or nearly! This made me realize that our plant had also changed a lot since the

---

* Terms followed by an asterisk are defined in the Glossary at the end of the book.

installation of our very first module. Every year we improve, and we change our methods a bit. Isn't that the *Kaizen** principle?

This volume is the fruit of my 30-year career as an industrial engineer, which I spent learning, analyzing, and observing the way TPS functions. *Lean Today, Rich Tomorrow: Succeeding in Today's Globalization Chaos* aims to be a practical, concrete work, presented in the form of a story told the way it was experienced. No complex formulas, no algorithms, no grand theories, and nothing at all that's overly technical. Just the process of a Canadian enterprise and its employees, and their successful implementation without the help of consultants, relying on only the sweat of their brows. The story of the Genfoot plant in Contrecoeur, Quebec—a story that continues in plants located in Ville St-Laurent, Quebec; New Hamburg, Ontario; and Littleton, New Hampshire. This is my story, and it's our story! Because, despite all the problems we encountered, the implementation of the Lean/TPS with JIT and *Kaizen* absolutely ensured our survival while many companies in our field fell under the shadow of bankruptcy.

I've tried, in this volume, to tell a tale of adventure and use a minimum of theory. However, to make it useful to both students and professionals, I had to explain the basic concepts of the Toyota system. I hope that the chapters that discuss mistakes along the way (Chapter 10), my tour of the Japanese plants (Chapter 16), and winning conditions (Chapter 14) will hold your interest. TPS is simple and it works like a charm! My internship in the Japanese plants fully convinced me. I hope that I, with my writing, can do the same for you. And I hope you'll enjoy reading this book as much as I enjoyed writing it.

Joe Bichai

Acknowledgments

Lean Today, Rich Tomorrow: Succeeding in Today's Globalization Chaos is my first and most likely my last book.

I would first like to thank the members of the Cook family, owners of the Genfoot company, who gave me their trust and provided me the opportunity to make my professional dream come true: to conduct a full implementation of a Lean manufacturing/JIT production system.

This major project could never have been carried out without the close collaboration of the plant manager, the late Monique Castonguay. I thank her sincerely for her support throughout the implementation. Her determination, willpower, and enthusiasm to see this culture change succeed greatly contributed to the success of the new approach.

I cannot forget the enormous contribution of our industrial engineer, Rita Manouk, who doubled her efforts at the start of the project and carried out a colossal amount of work. Her technical assistance, dynamic approach, and persistence in carrying out new challenges inspired all the employees, and I am grateful for that. Other collaborators at the Montreal head office also directly and indirectly helped with the implementation's success, including Evelyne Belleau, Liliane LeBel, and Sylvie Michaud, as well as Arold Isaac and Christian Lecavalier. I thank them as well. I am also very grateful to all the employees of the Contrecoeur factory, and later, those of the St-Laurent, New Hamburg, and Littleton sites who trusted us and agreed to experiment with us. Without their participation and their sacrifices, the implementation would have failed.

I also thank the entire team at the Centre d'étude des interactions biologiques entre la santé et l'environnement (CINBIOSE), including Nicole Vézina and Pierre-Paul Bilodeau, for their involvement in the project. I want to express my warmest thanks to everyone who believed in my idea and helped me put together this book, including Les Presses Internationales Polytechnique—particularly Constance Forest, editor of the initial French version of the book, for her valuable help, Luce Venne-Forcione, and Andrea Zanin, who translated it into English.

Finally, I would like to express my deep gratitude to my wife and children. I was often unavailable to them during the first two years of the implementation; as well, for those two years they spent their vacation time watching me write. I must admit that writing this book reached the level of obsession for me, which pretty much ruined family holidays!

About the Author

Joe Bichai is recognized and looked upon as a leader in the world of Lean manufacturing. Throughout his career he has enthusiastically shared his knowledge of Lean and continuous improvement philosophy. Committed to the success of domestic manufacturing, he has conducted numerous seminars and taught future grads how to be competitive in our global markets.

After graduating from the Ecole Polytechnique de Montréal as an industrial engineer, Bichai joined Electrolux as a young and eager engineer. He worked his way through the ranks and was promoted to I.E. manager, later to manufacturing engineering manager and to finally plant manager. In 1986, he decided to start his own company, JITECH Manufacturing Services, offering his customers, a one-stop shop for manufacturers looking for plastic molds as well as molded and assembled products.

In 1991, he seized the opportunity to partner up with Kamik (Genfoot Inc.), the leading Canadian footwear manufacturer. Since then, Bichai has been leading the manufacturing activities of their three North American factories.

In 1998, the CSIE (Canadian Society for Industrial Engineering) awarded him the Leadership award for promoting Canadian productivity.

In 2000, he was awarded "the most influential engineer of his decade" award by the Ecole Polytechnique de Montréal's industrial engineering department.

For the past 30 years, Bichai has been a proud advocate of the Japanese manufacturing management techniques that led him in 2001 to join the Gemba Kaizen and Just-in-Time study tour at the Japan Kaizen Institute, where he perfected his continuous improvement knowledge learning from Imai Masaaki, founder of the Kaizen Institute.

In 2007, Bichai's French version book *Agir ou Périr* was published by the Presses Internationales de Polytechnique and was selected as a finalist in the annual Quebec Better Business Book Grand Prix competition.

Introduction
An Idea That's Making Its Mark

NOVEMBER 1982

I'm reading my first book on the Toyota Production System* (TPS) and from this point onward, the Toyota system fascinates me, even to the point of obsession. At the time, I am a young industrial engineer with three years' experience working in the production department of Electrolux®, a vacuum cleaner manufacturer. I find it difficult to imagine that it's possible to produce an automobile, an object of such complexity, 10 times larger than a vacuum cleaner, in such little time and with such an exceptional level of quality, with no work in process. The author talks about *kanban**, a mysterious system of production control cards. Could this really be superior to our MRP* system? Is it really possible to produce using a pull system* with versatile employees who work completely autonomously, on U-shaped production lines? How can they be responsible for the maintenance of their own machines? Even our maintenance technicians often have a lot of trouble diagnosing problems with our injection machines. The author must surely be exaggerating.

That said, I really like the base concept of just in time* (JIT*), even if its implementation seems pretty risky to me. I discuss it with my colleagues and decide to make a presentation on the topic to management.

The reaction is unanimous: "That's fantastic!... Except that Japanese culture is totally different from ours! It's a stock reduction and quality improvement process," they said.

"You should mention this to the union reps," says the production director cynically. "I'd love to see their reaction to your proposal to have an injection machine operator work several machines, as well as doing the maintenance for them!" He adds, "You know, in the end, this would mean a reduced number of union workers, an increase in workload, and an end to the bonus system based on number of units produced. Good luck!"

JUST IN TIME, *KANBAN*, AND MRP IN BRIEF

While many people confuse JIT with *kanban*, the distinction between the two is significant, although simple. JIT is a production management philosophy, while *kanban* is a control tool for that production and for the movement of goods in process. *Kanban,* among other things, eliminates overproduction. The concept is fantastically simple but its effectiveness is without comparison. During a trip to the United States in the 1950s, Taiichi Ohno, the Japanese industrial engineer who came up with the TPS, was inspired by what he observed in a supermarket. He noticed that the store shelves displaying products to customers presented a very limited stocking capacity, but that when the stock hit a low level, a clerk would restock the shelves. In a way, the customers were "pulling" the products from the warehouse or the supplier. This is the origin of the concept of a pull system. The MRP system, or Materials Requirements Planning, in turn, appeared in the United Sates in the early 1960s. The concept then evolved to become Manufacturing Resources Planning* that we know today. The system first evaluates the company's capacities based on sales forecasts and generates a production plan. Then, starting with the product's Bill of Material (BOM), it determines the components to buy or produce in keeping with the production plan.

My boss immediately takes a more conciliatory and encouraging approach, while nevertheless pointing out that there are major differences between the cultures of the two countries and that in Japan, you get a job for life in exchange for unconditional devotion to the employer, exemplary discipline, and respect for authority. With that, I conclude that it would be impossible for me to change anything in my company, and that maybe they have a point. After all, these are experienced people talking. So I resign myself to accepting their recommendations, even though I am convinced that with a good training plan and a good management team, we could implement the philosophy. I promise myself that I'll further investigate this cultural difference and perhaps come up with responses to the objections that arose.

Starting now, I undertake to research everything that's been published on the topic. One year and six books later, I conclude that for such a transformation to succeed, it must be initiated from the top-down, and it also must be understood by every member of the organization. If you don't get unconditional commitment from upper management, the project has no chance of success. This condition is key to gaining the cooperation and total devotion of each individual involved in a process that is actually pretty simple, but long-lasting, and that has no room for shortcuts.

Chapter 1

Ten Years Later

JUNE 1991

I clearly remember the somewhat extraordinary circumstances through which I ended up at Genfoot. A recruiter specializing in senior management head-hunting, whom I'd known for a few years, calls me to talk about the company. He knows my professional experience is a good match for his client's needs, and that the offer might well interest me. The senior management includes the president (son of the founder), his right hand and executive vice president, as well as his three sons in their thirties—vice presidents of finance, sales, and overseas operations. They're looking to fill the position of vice president of manufacturing for their injection plant. Doubtless, my dozen years' experience in the field of molds and plastics molding is of great interest to them.

GENFOOT IN BRIEF

Genfoot Inc. is the Canadian footwear industry leader. In 1991, this vertically integrated family business operates three plants in North America: an injection plant located in the head-office building in Saint-Laurent, a Montreal suburb, which manufactures winter boots and bottoms; a factory in New Hamburg, Ontario, that makes the various felts they use for linings; and finally, a cutting and sewing factory located in Contrecoeur, north of Montreal. The latter two have been in operation since 1898, so for nearly 115 years. The Contrecoeur factory reports to the executive vice president, who mostly takes care of international sales. As for the director of the felt factory in Ontario, he reports to the company president.

After doing some research on Genfoot and the shoe industry in Canada, I decide to take a pass on the offer. There's absolutely nothing reassuring in the industry—in the previous five years, 45 businesses have gone under, resulting in the loss of 6,000 jobs. The scenario seems to be the same in most cases: low productivity, outdated equipment, quality problems, and fierce competition from Mexico, the Dominican Republic, and Asia. That said, against this somber backdrop, Genfoot is an exception: its specialization in high-quality outdoor boot manufacturing, as well as very tight financial management, has allowed the company to emerge with a strong profit margin. The company has an excellent reputation even beyond Canada's borders, considering it exports over 60% of its production to the United States, Europe, and Japan. As well, it devotes a good portion of its budget to research and development projects. However, the company never takes major risks and isn't diversifying its products into areas beyond outdoor footwear gear; it only produces winter boots, hunting boots, hiking boots, rain boots, and sports sandals.

Things could have stopped there but I tell the recruiter that since our last conversation five years earlier, I've started my own business in the field of subcontracting for molds and technical parts molding for the automobile, electronics, and aerospace markets; in fact, when the Electrolux plant closed, I seized the opportunity to make my entrepreneurship dream come true with the help of two other engineers. When he learns this, the recruiter, a shrewd and tenacious fellow, won't let up: he's convinced I am the perfect candidate for the job at Genfoot. So he suggests that his client consider the possibility of a guaranteed partnership, knowing that without this possibility, I'll have no interest in meeting him. Although *a priori* Genfoot is looking for an experienced manager and not a partner, we undertake discussions and after a number of conversations, a meeting is set up for me with the company leaders. The meeting is set for 8:30 a.m. on Monday morning.

All weekend, I think about the meeting—not about whether or not I'm interested in the job itself, but I'm drawn to the idea of discovering a new world, an industry that's completely new to me.

Monday morning, I show up at 8:20 a.m. (I'd rather be an hour early to a meeting than a minute late). At 8:30 a.m., the company owner, Gordon Cook, meets me at the reception desk and guides me toward the conference room. Two of his sons, Rick and Steve, as well as an in-house consultant, Gerry Dolan, are waiting there. The only person missing is the executive vice president Vic, an early riser who, to everyone's surprise, has still not shown up at the office this morning. After the usual introductions, when we have been sitting down for just a minute, the receptionist shows up at the conference room door. She asks the president to take an important call. He tells her, politely, to please take a message. "Sir," she insists, "I think you should take it. It's Vic's son (the executive vice president) and he absolutely needs to speak with you." Gordon excuses himself. He comes back five minutes later, his face pale and sad. The executive vice president, his right-hand man, his friend of 40 years, almost a brother, passed away a few hours earlier. Everyone in the conference room is dismayed, and I feel very awkward. At the first opportunity, I offer my condolences to the president and suggest we put off our discussion to a more opportune time. Nothing about it is urgent, I tell myself. But contrary to what I expect, the president asks me to give him a few minutes to make a number of calls, and says he would still like to take the time to bring me on a tour of the two factories that day. Gerry, the consultant, offers to take me right away to the injection plant, which is located in the same building as the head office; the tour should take 45 minutes and we could continue our interview directly afterward. So I follow him through the hallway to the staircase leading to the factory. Gerry is a gentleman the likes of which I have rarely encountered. Also, as an engineer who had retired several years ago, he had spent some 50 years in the shoe industry and is a veritable walking encyclopedia of the field. At Gordon Cook's request, he joined the company eight years ago, at age 66. He mostly takes care of R&D activities but also advises engineering and production staff on all aspects of manufacturing.

I'm looking forward to touring the plant, injection molding being my strength. When I see the first machine, my jaw hits the floor. I had never seen an injection machine that looks anything like this monstrosity. It's a rotating injection machine with 10 to 14 stations that each holds a pair of boots in a given size. Every 30 seconds, an operator pulls a boot out of its steel mold. Most machines are equipped with two injection barrels; some have three, to inject different compounds for the sole and the top part, called the upper. Hanging from an overhead conveyor, the boots cool down. I'm afraid of my guide's reaction to my surprise because the recruiter had praised my merits in the plastics field. But Gerry says not to worry if I've never seen anything of the sort. These molds and machines, made in Italy, are truly unique, both in their design and in their operation. We then move to another section, where chemical products are mixed. Another very rare case in the plastics industry, Genfoot manufactures all the thermoplastic resins it injects. This makes it possible for them to design products that meet their customers' very precise needs, and to set the company apart from its competitors, who all have to buy their thermoplastic resins from the same suppliers. I still try to impress him by talking about just-in-time, quick mold change, and total quality. He listens to me quite attentively.

We go up to meet with the other management team members and continue our discussions. We talk about my past experience and my career goals. Later, Gordon insists on taking me to tour the Contrecoeur cutting and sewing factory, the company's "crown jewel." The factory alone produces more than 60% of Genfoot's total sales, in eight months out of the year. I'm asked to wait momentarily at reception to be driven to Contrecoeur.

For these few minutes' break, I can't help but think about everything that's happened since 8:30 a.m. this morning. I tell myself I might be seen as a bad omen, but what had happened might also change many things. In no time, the company had become more vulnerable than ever, and for that very reason, the position of vice president of manufacturing might take on a whole new level of importance and become even more interesting to me. In short, I was in the right place at the right time.

Because the company is vertically integrated, I don't understand how the directors of the three factories could report to three different executives. If they all reported to the same management, in this case the vice president of manufacturing, the company could function more easily in a just-in-time environment.

The president, who finds the time to smile at me, gestures for me to follow him. I persist in telling him I'd be happy to come back another day but as far as he's concerned, there's no question about it: he insists that we visit the Contrecoeur factory.

We start the drive. I take the opportunity to ask the president about the deceased and his role in the Contrecoeur factory. Isn't he in charge of sales? Why doesn't the vice president of manufacturing take care of that? While we chat and the farms roll by outside the window, I wonder again what I'm doing here. After my tour this morning, I'm even less interested by the field. Also, what do I know about sewing, apart from having seen my mother use her sewing machine at home?

We arrive at the factory, where we're greeted by the director, who, like Gerry Dolan, left retirement to give the president a hand. The news of Vic's death has already reached the factory, and Gordon fields questions from every direction.

We finally enter the ground-floor production area, and I see a worrisome sight. The factory is packed with cardboard boxes of every size. I also see conveyors on which plastic boxes filled with leather and nylon pieces move from a central distribution post to the seamstresses, who sit at various points near the conveyor, sewing all sorts of pieces at top speed. There are a total of four identical raw-material conveyors, differentiated only by the model of boot being made. Some 40 seamstresses are each performing a single operation at a time, and bringing the baskets back to the single distribution point. It's difficult to get your bearings, as each seamstress could work on a different boot model. This mode of operation is totally different from a production line, where each operation follows the next and each one brings added value. As well, it's difficult to see all the workers because some seamstresses are surrounded by boxes, practically buried under products that are part way through the manufacturing process (i.e., work in process). In all the mayhem, a few handlers are trying to forge paths for themselves by pushing a first dolly of half-finished boots with one hand while pulling a second dolly with the other.

In front of each conveyor, there are also a hundred other boxes that have come down from the upper floors. The second floor is where the felt, leather, and nylon are cut; once the pieces are cut, they're sent to the ground floor, where they accumulate. I understand right away that the cutters, also paid on a piecework basis, have no reason to slow down their production, even if the cut pieces are overflowing on the next floor. This is the kind of problem that any push system* creates for production. Every man for himself, and bonuses for everyone!

In a corner, I notice something strange. Instead of sewing boots, a dozen employees are busy picking the stitches out! The plant manager, who had proudly pointed out the quality of the products his factory produced and boasted of zero defects, explains that this is the rework department. These employees make sure that no defective boot leaves the factory. I admit they do excellent work, but I am floored! Didn't they just pay someone to sew the boot? Why pay another one to repair the work done by a first, less-conscientious person?

During this time, I see people milling about empty-handed, as well as finishing workers (the final operation before packaging) who are putting laces and labels on boots. The boots are then placed on six-foot-tall shelf trolleys, with a one-foot space between each shelf. I can't help but think about my ergonomics professor when I see a woman bent in half to lace up boots on the bottom shelf, while a second, on the other side of the trolley, is stretching up on tiptoe to do the same on the top shelf.

The final inspection is conducted at the packaging station. Three two-person teams inspect and package the finished products. Nothing gets through unless the product is perfectly in keeping with the customer's requirements. In general, the more demanding the customer, the busier the rework department gets.

Once my tour is finished, we head back to Montreal. I can't help thinking about my much-loved Lean*/Toyota JIT system. The more I think about it, the more I see major advantages in applying it to the footwear industry. I am convinced that with JIT and a good-quality program, Genfoot could eliminate all the problems I just saw. But come to think of it, did anyone talk to me about problems? Not to my knowledge. On the contrary, everyone I met sang the praises of their production system.

The fatal question comes up quickly. "Joe, what do you think of the factory?" asks Gordon.

"Um, I've never toured a shoe factory before this one, but do they all work like that?"

"Yes, but some don't have conveyors like ours. We've greatly improved our productivity since we installed them."

A few seconds of silence elapse before my next question. "Do you make money with this factory?"

"Of course we make money. It's our biggest factory. We have excellent specialized workers who take the company's success to heart. All our employees are from the area. The steel plants employ the local men, and we employ their wives. I'm very proud of what we've accomplished here but we can always improve. I'm guessing from your questions that you have ideas in mind."

Phew! I'm reassured! He's aware that they could do better. I still haven't said what I think of the factory but I feel a little more at ease. I still don't know if I should be polite and make him happy by saying I'm impressed, or be frank and direct. My brief hesitation makes him speak up again.

"Don't try to make me happy. I want to hear what you really think."

"Okay, here's what I think. You have a beautiful factory with very good employees who work at a crazy rate and produce good quality but, personally, I've always been against piecework. Nobody can convince me that we can produce the best possible quality working by piece rate. When I was at Electrolux, I used to set the production standards with the MTM (Methods-Time-Measurement*) system. We were constantly fighting with the operators and their union for each new standard. They never really understood the concept of a learning curve."

"So what would you suggest for improving my productivity?"

Now I'm a bit stuck. If I say that in his best factory, things are working all wrong and I have no solutions to offer, I'm the one who'll look really stupid! So I simply ask him if he's heard of the Lean manufacturing or just-in-time method. It's unlikely, from what I can see, that he has, because he's never worked in production. To my great surprise, he asks me, "Isn't that the system implemented by Toyota and applied by just about everyone these days?"

I think to myself, fantastic! We're going to understand each other! He tells me that the *Wall Street Journal*, his favorite newspaper, has published several articles on JIT. I tell him everything I know on the subject and pique his curiosity. He's pretty impressed and wants to know what I'd do if I had the opportunity. So I don't hold back. I answer, "I'd get rid of the piecework and the supply conveyors. I'd put a quality system in place. I'd reconfigure the current factory layout to create one that would facilitate process convergence. I'd organize a number of small U-shaped production cells, where a multi-disciplinary team would assemble a pair of boots from A to Z. And I'd manufacture products only after receiving a customer order. That's what we call a pull production system. There you go! That's probably what the *Wall Street Journal* was talking about!" I conclude.

The last time I'd spoken this way, I had been ridiculed, and my ego had taken a beating. But that was 10 years ago. In the interim, I had acquired more experience and learned a lot by founding my own business, JITECH Manufacturing Services (JITECH for Just-In-Time Technologies). So this time, I'm ready to defend each of the points I just listed. But I don't need to. In fact, Gordon is enchanted with the idea. Still a little worried, however, he wonders: do we have the internal resources to pull off this kind of project?

We had arrived in St-Laurent a few minutes ago, so we shake hands and promise to be in touch again near the end of the week. No need to rush things; I'm well aware that Gordon's next few days will be difficult ones, what with the funeral home, the funeral ceremonies, and the board of directors' emergency meeting. And on my end, after a very full day, it's now time for me to do some serious thinking about my future. As they say, I need to sleep on it.

Chapter 2

Setting the Challenge

JULY 1991

Despite my reservations—I have to mourn the high-tech industrial milieu I'm used to in order to move into a more low-tech environment—I agree to join Genfoot, stimulated by the challenge it offers. Also, the president's receptivity to my reorganization ideas opens the doors for me to apply *Kaizen** in an industrial setting, which I've dreamed of experiencing for 10 years now!

But the work is just beginning. I'm standing in the middle of the Contrecoeur factory—the biggest footwear factory in Canada!—and the picture hasn't changed since my visit the previous month. The production floor is so packed with all kinds of raw materials and work in process that it's difficult for me to walk around safely. That said, once I'm in the action, I realize that all the great ideas I had talked about during my interview will be a lot more complicated to implement than I'd ever thought. I mean, where do I begin? How do I convince the employees to change their way of working when they're happy with their work conditions? How do I justify to the company's executives that it's wise to shake up things like this when the factory is turning a profit? In other words, why fix something that's not broken and that's satisfying the two parties concerned?

From management's point of view, the status quo is easy to explain. Genfoot is effectively blinded by its own success. Some bad work habits, some obsolete procedures, and a traditional management philosophy are accepted because they guarantee peace with the employees while meeting the business's short-term growth objective. But what will happen in the long term? With the arrival of free trade (the North American Free Trade Agreement, or NAFTA) and market globalization, our competitors are no longer across the street or just over the American border; they're on the other side of the world! And whether they're in China or Mexico, one thing is for sure: their labor costs are a fraction of ours.

In the past, to determine a product's sale price, we just had to calculate the cost, add a profit, and Bob's your uncle!

$$\text{Sale price} = \text{Cost} + \text{Profit} \qquad (2.1)$$

This practice no longer works today. The concept of a market price set by our customers has replaced that of cost plus profit. In fact, in many cases, our customer imposes the sale price on us because the customer can get a supply from a competitor anywhere in the world at a lower price. The best example is that of a model we've been making for some 10 years: we're selling it to the same customer today at a lower price than we were a decade ago! If we add inflation and increased labor costs, of course our productivity has to get better every year to compensate. If we get our employees on board to work with *Kaizen* principles, we could make major improvements. To get there, we need to show them where we're falling short, expose the hidden problems in our current system, and lead them to take part in the change that needs to happen.

Because the plant manager is now officially retired, I take the opportunity to offer the job to Monique Castonguay, an employee with more than 20 years' seniority who has risen through the ranks because she's dynamic, professional, and assertive. Unlike her predecessor, she clearly realizes that we absolutely must improve our competitiveness if we want to survive in an industry that's short on good news these days. Together, we decide to take the rest of the current season to cook up our plan.

Faced with a gigantic project, Monique and I decide to prioritize the hiring of a good industrial engineer. Rita Manouk is the first engineer of any specialty who's ever been hired in this nearly100-year-old factory. Although it's overstuffed with workers, machines, and materials, the factory is a true paradise for an industrial engineer. Every time we take student engineers on a tour, they're very impressed with what they see. All the theory courses they take at university are put into practice here, right before their eyes. Their class materials on work, handling, layout, planning, quality control, and ergonomics—it's all here! It's pretty incredible that a factory this big has managed to go without an industrial engineer for this long when having one would have helped them avoid a number of the problems I've listed. But it's never too late to do it right!

Monique and I throw ourselves into developing a list of the problems we see in the production area. The list gets longer every day, and six months later, we decide we have enough ammo to call an unusual kind of employee meeting in order to present them with a picture of the industry and our situation.

We decide to hold the gathering in the city's community hall. Apart from the municipal arena, it's the only possible choice because the factory doesn't have a room big enough to hold 350 people.

When the unusual meeting is announced, the rumor machine wastes no time kicking into high gear. "The factory is closing" is the most popular story! Other people are talking about massive layoffs to make room for imported products. There are no positive rumors. Right then and there, I tell myself that if the rumors are so negative, surely that's because the employees recognize that something's not quite working! That said, I think it may be the first time that factory management has called a meeting like this, so it makes sense that they might be worried about it. In the past, when Monique had an important message to convey, she gathered the employees at the foot of the staircase separating the factory from the offices, stood at the top of the staircase and spoke loudly enough for everyone to hear her. To see and hear her properly, each person had to pick their way between boxes of goods in process and find a little spot to stand.

AN ANALYSIS OF THE SITUATION

The next sections cover what we present to our employees on the morning of July 30, 1992.

Economic Context of the Shoe Industry in Canada

First we describe the key points of the situation for Canadian shoe companies:

- The industry has lost 6,000 jobs and 45 companies in the past six years (1985–1991).
- Retailers can get a supply of shoes from China and Mexico for a fraction of the manufacturing cost of Canadian businesses.
- The local industry's spending on occupational health and safety (OHS) keeps growing, to the detriment of profits.
- Overall productivity in Canadian factories leaves much to be desired.

State of Our Factory

We next present a summary of the situation in our factory. We project a series of photos taken on-site, in the heat of the action, which helps us bring our employees' attention to a few anomalies. The most obvious ones are the following (see Photo 2.1):

- Each seamstress sitting in front of her machine is surrounded by boxes piled up all over the place around her.
- The amount of work in process is very high.
- The factory is bogged down with stock pile-ups* (see Photo 2.2).
- We're flooded with defective components.
- The layout is awful, typical of a work environment for a push system.

---

* The space problem is so pronounced that expansion plans were already approved. Thanks to our close ties with the municipality, the municipal zoning bylaw was amended so we could use the employee parking lot for the expansion.

PHOTO 2.1 Seamstresses arrayed around a conveyor.

PHOTO 2.2 Production space jammed with a pile-up of goods in process.

As well, we point out other problems, less visible but still omnipresent:

- It takes 15 to 25 days to produce an order.
- One department is devoted entirely to repairing defective products.
- There are no engineering standards, meaning scientifically defined time measures, for operation cycles.
- We can see attitude problems related to piecework, such as individualism.
- Some employees are lacking in motivation.
- There is no sense of belonging in regard to the company.

To remain competitive and ensure the company's survival, we have to eliminate all the bad work habits and organization problems, starting with

- Piecework, which generates poor quality by placing the emphasis on quantity
- Banking*, which throws off our production reports
- The rework department, which masks procedure problems
- Buffer inventory that's much too high, and that burdens the company's budget
- Production lots that are too big, which hide operation planning problems
- Handling dollies, which clog up the workspace
- Rejects, which require repairs and increase production costs
- Inventory shortages, which delay our deliveries
- A high rate of absenteeism

In short, we need to change everything, including the factory's layout.

THE SOLUTION: TOYOTA'S LEAN PRODUCTION SYSTEM AND *KAIZEN*

Faced with this situation, we can't help but note that we need a serious shake-up. And for us, there is only one option: Toyota's Lean* system and *Kaizen*. So we take the time to explain what these systems are to our employees and to promote their merits, while cautioning everyone against the discouragement that might come up while they're being implemented. Because even if these new ways of working open up our horizons, putting them into place is a giant challenge to carry out for any business that wants to head in that direction.

Where to Begin?

We continue our exposé by adding that, to guide us in our implementation process, we first have to define a mission that's worthy of a world-class factory. We present the one we've come up with.

_____
* I discuss banking in more detail in Chapter 3, Module Section.

To create a new "quality" culture in the organization, meaning that

- Our employees must
  - Be versatile
  - Work in self-managed teams
  - Work on small production lots
  - Operate in well-defined modules (cells) to produce superior-quality boots in very short time frames
- This will have the effect of increasing
  - Motivation and self-esteem among workers
  - Productivity

All this takes place within a continued improvement process.

The expressions on the employees' faces tell me that most likely the only two messages they've retained are that not only is the industry in danger—and therefore so are their jobs—but also that we need to change our work habits. All the benefits of JIT* and *Kaizen* have gone way over their heads. I also understand that they're shaken but I'm not overly worried about it because we have a lot of time ahead of us to go over the project in detail.

Our Way of Working

The process we propose to the employees is simple: we have to experiment together. We'll learn, act, and decide TOGETHER!

We'll assemble an experimental team with a few volunteer cutters, seamstresses, and packers. That team will try to develop and standardize a new work method to be used by all the factory's workers. The volunteers must be experienced employees, strong communicators, and ready to work in a team. They'll be pulled from production for an undetermined period and will have to work standing up.

Monique and I had worried that we wouldn't get any volunteers. In that case, we'd planned to have to convince a few employees one by one to try the experiment, and possibly even pay them a little bonus to encourage them. But surprisingly, a number of employees—more than we needed, in fact—are waiting for us at the end of the meeting to tell us they intend to volunteer. They don't even seem concerned about how they'll get paid!

To end the meeting, we agree on a three-month trial period, during which we'll measure a number of parameters and manufacturing activities and compare the results from the experimental module with the ones we get using the traditional production approach. Among others, we'll analyze

- Work in process
- Reject rate
- Surface area used
- Manufacturing lead time
- Efficiency (performance)

The volunteer employees will form a new committee. Every day, they'll have discussions among themselves and with management (meaning the plant manager Monique, the newly hired industrial engineer Rita Manouk, and me) about the way the experimental module is working.

At the end of three months, we'll meet again with all the employees in the same place, and we'll share the results we've obtained and the new committee's recommendations.

And on that note, we end the meeting.

Chapter 3

Rethinking the Factory's Layout and Production Philosophy

At the first meeting of the newly formed implementation committee, we have to decide on where to put the pilot module, the product that it manufactures, and the roles and responsibilities of each of its members. At this stage of the project, a number of participants are in training to better tackle their new roles.

On our end, we've decided to give minimal direction. Really, we want to let problems come up so that we act in consequence and can provide more appropriate and better targeted training as a result. So I describe this new management philosophy to the new committee over a half-day, without getting into too much detail, and we let them start experimenting right away as a team.

THE MODULE: A PRODUCTION NERVE CENTER

The module is at the core of the factory work method we want to implement. So it's of crucial importance that we put in all the energy we need in order to design it properly.

The Design and Setup of the Pilot Module

We want to isolate the pilot module from the rest of production, such that we don't interfere with the factory's activities; but above all, we want to create a certain intrigue and pique the other employees' curiosity about this new way of working. The placement choice lands on a room located on the first floor that currently warehouses small accessories such as laces, grommets, and so forth. Poster board carefully pasted over the door's two windows hides the inside of the room from view, to make sure the pilot group isn't disturbed, while also maintaining the mystery.

We also study the choice of product to manufacture there. After a few discussions, we opt for a model we call the duck shoe. It's one of the simplest to produce. This choice helps us pare down the variables related to the complexity of the product. Really, we have so many unknowns in this project that we're looking to eliminate the nonessential variables as much as possible in an effort to focus on the ones that result from the experiment itself. For example, sewing a piece, whether it's made of nylon or leather, or whether it's done on this machine or that one, remains an act of sewing! However, the choice of a pedal, the placement of the connections, the height of the machines, and so forth are all important to analyze.

In the experiment room, the conveyor will disappear; a shoe will move from one place to the next from hand-to-hand, based on the one-piece flow* system. Because the advantage of a module is flexibility and the ease of manufacturing in small quantities, we decide to design and standardize it in order to optimize the number of modules per surface unit based on the quantities to be produced. Because we only have work in process as stock, the module will occupy a smaller area than for traditional manufacturing*. As well, because the module's employees are empowered, that will boost their motivation and result in better product quality at a more competitive cost.

We place a small shelving unit at the module's entrance for everyday needs in leather and nylon. The cutter uses a shelf on the unit to store various sizes of dies to cut. After the cutting comes the addition of a serial number or traceability code. After the traditional sewing process comes the addition of trim and insole, the assembly of the upper to the rubber bottom, and the packaging of the finished product. Figure 3.1 illustrates the setup we chose.

Because sewing with a single Pfaff® 335 machine causes a bottleneck, we decide to install two of these machines. Between the gluing table and operation 335, we set up a space for the shoe bottoms coming from the Montreal factory. Once these operations are done, the product is finished and packed on-site, ready for delivery to the customer.

Choosing a U-Shaped Module

After considering several possibilities, we opt for a U-shaped module. U-shaped modular manufacturing* offers a number of advantages, the most significant of which are

- The entrance of raw materials and the exit of finished products are side-by-side.
- This setup facilitates communication between employees, which helps with problem solving.
- The number of employees working in it can be adapted as needed.

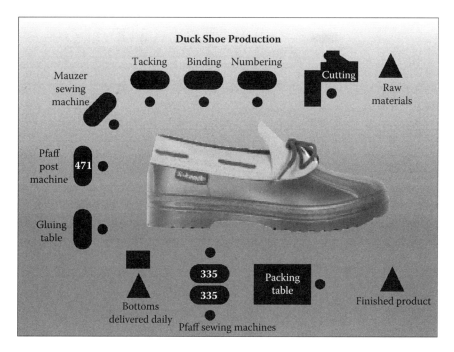

FIGURE 3.1 Layout of the pilot module.

From having tried it, I can assure you that this is the shape all modules should take.

To better understand what the U-shaped module and group technology* represent in terms of improvement, let's take a look, by comparison, at the traditional way of manufacturing this same product in our factory.

TRADITIONAL ORGANIZATION
AND MANUFACTURING METHODS

The Contrecoeur factory building seems more like a school than a factory. It has three floors and a basement, which in itself creates problems with supply circulation, communication, and overall activity control. It has been expanded twice over the course of its 100-year existence without any lasting solution to these organizational problems.

The raw material arrives every day from our Montreal warehouse. The leather and nylon are sent by elevator to the third floor for stocking. The rolls of felt are taken to the basement, while the rubber bottoms are kept on the same floor as the shipping/receiving area, meaning the ground floor (Figure 3.2).

Leather and nylon are cut on the second floor. The cutters, mostly men, are paid by the piece as well as receiving a performance bonus averaging 30% to 40%. The leather, spread across the clicker press table, is cut one piece at a time using a die, which allows the cutter to check the quality before moving to the next step. The nylon, for its part, is cut in several layers, varying

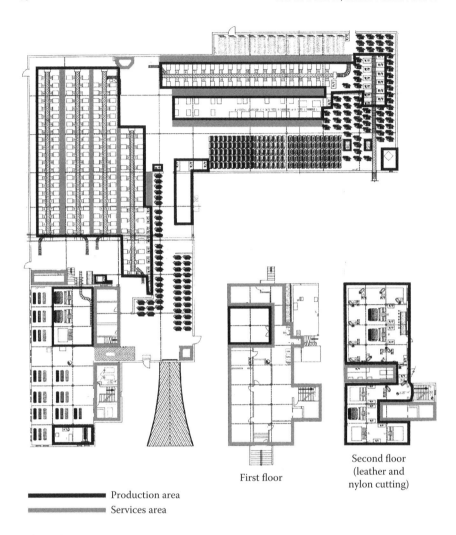

Second floor
(leather and
First floor   nylon cutting)

▬▬▬▬▬ Production area
▨▨▨▨▨ Services area

FIGURE 3.2 Traditional factory layout. The area used for added-value production only represents one third of the total available area.

between 24 and 64 depending on its thickness. This work uses a taller, wider press. The foreman on duty always brags of having the best-performing department in the factory.

The felt cutters, in turn, work in the basement and use presses similar to the ones used for nylon but they cut eight layers of felt at a time. It goes without saying that they, too, are paid by piecework. Like their colleagues on the second floor, they post efficiency rates of over 130%. The lots cut ahead of time are sent by conveyor to the ground floor where the sewing takes place. Because they're focused above all on the quantity they're producing—to say nothing of their bonuses—the cutters and their foremen aren't the least bit concerned about the problems they cause on the sewing floor. The ground-floor

PHOTO 3.1 Partial view of four component conveyors and the lots coming from the cutters.

production area is so overflowing with raw materials that show up too early and in too large a quantity that handlers were hired to put away the materials. Hundreds of boxes containing pieces of leather, nylon, and felt are stocked in the four corners of the factory before they end up on the main manufacturing conveyors. Five such conveyors specialize in assembling one or another of these materials (Photo 3.1). And the push production* mode has no solution for this whole mess.

Scattered near the conveyors, hundreds of seamstresses sit in front of their machines and ceaselessly perform *one single* operation per piece before sending the lots they produce back to the departure point. Then, a production stocker gives them more raw materials as quickly as possible. Sophisticated conveyors automatically deliver a container of one or more piece lots to wherever an indicator is flashing.

The operators, mostly seamstresses, deposit the empty containers on the bottom shelf of the conveyor. They take care to remove the little coupons attached to each lot to be produced, because they represent the salary for the operation they've performed. At the end of the workday, each operator can add together their coupons and calculate exactly what they'll be paid.

Production standards haven't been revised for several years, and they are based on those of similar models produced in the past. As in any factory that encourages piecework, the employees are the first to complain when the standards are difficult to reach or exceed. But of course, nobody says a word when they're too low or haven't been checked in a long time.

Our factory is no different from any other in this sense; however, the unusual thing with us is that our employees aren't obliged to hand in all the coupons they accumulate at the end of the day, or the week, or the month. They can keep them and cash them in anytime they feel like it. This is where the concept of *banking* originates. This word, used often in our factory, refers to an amount of "banked" money, meaning an amount due for work performed but that has not yet been paid. This amount can exceed $100,000 for the factory workers as a whole. For employees, banking represents security. They know they have a little financial cushion in their pocket that they can draw on as needed to get additional pay. A seamstress explains quite simply that when she's not in top shape and doesn't perform at her best, she can pull out a few coupons from her reserves to compensate for her loss. The more questions I ask about banking, the more aberrant I find the practice! What surprises me the most is that the employees are so attached to it that they have threatened to strike in the past when my predecessor wanted to put an end to it. As an employer, they say, I shouldn't complain. The company is making interest on the amount they hold on to, and ends up with a carryover that can range from $25,000 to $50,000 of unclaimed pay at the end of each fiscal year! However, the system isn't always a beneficial one for the employees because the coupons get lost, torn, or even stolen, such that some workers never get their due. Another absurdity: I even heard it said that the local bar accepted payment in our coupons when one of our employees couldn't pay his entire bill! He could easily find someone who'd agree to cash them in at the factory for him!

Our biggest problem with this practice is that all the production reports that have been presented to me are completely wrong. Employees could be sitting and playing cards in the cafeteria while declaring 130% efficiency for the day. They'd just need to take out enough coupons from their pockets to represent the amount they wanted to cash in. That means that as long as the coupons aren't cashed in, the true production rate can't be known. You can surely imagine all the problems that might cause...

Let's get back to our seamstresses, who carry out one operation at a time on a lot that's sent to them. When we analyze each of their movements, it's clear that they spend more time handling the piece than they do adding value to it: taking it from the left, placing it in front of the machine, sewing for a few seconds, picking it up, and depositing it in a box to the right.

Another problem: there's no link between the seamstresses who sit next to one another along the conveyor. It's nothing like a production chain, where each employee carries out a task on a given piece and then passes it to the next person. Instead, a single box might make the rounds of the conveyor several times while a given part of a shoe is prepared. As a concrete example, let's take a leather shaft (also called an upper) on which we need to sew a small crest, do some embroidery, and install a lace, D-rings, and plastic trim. To carry out all these operations, the same container might go around the conveyor four or five times.

Four conveyors serve to move containers for the production of leather and nylon uppers, while a fifth is reserved for the sewing of felt linings. Like the leather and nylon or felt cutters who push their production toward the sewing

PHOTO 3.2 Boxes of felt linings cut and sewn ahead of time.

conveyors, the employees who sew the felt push the pieces they produce toward the ground-floor assembly conveyor. Once sewn, the felt is stocked along a wall while waiting to be used when the boots are being finished. The seamstresses, in fact, have to use little stickers from a fabric roll, called Tyvex®, to indicate the size and composition of the felt pieces. Imagine my surprise when I see the seamstresses taking these little rolled-up stickers out of their bras! By "storing" them this way, they save time and can beat the daily standard. A silly thought crosses my mind: what engineer could write an MTM* standard specifying a "reach" to bra followed by a "grasp" of Tyvex and a "move"!

Unbelievable what piecework can do!

We can always count on having 1,000 to 1,500 boxes of felt linings cut and sewn, waiting for stickers, which take up an area of nearly 2,000 square feet (Photo 3.2). The felt linings manufacturing department even has "searchers," whose job is to find, in the factory, the boxes of linings that correspond to the boots in production on the chain!

The bottom and the upper are then assembled on the last conveyor. When the sewn boots arrive at the end of the conveyor, they're deposited on wheeled multi-shelf units near the place where finishing is done. This step consists of first slipping the felt lining into the boot, and then adding laces and hang tags for product identification. To do this, the employees—mostly women and of different heights—have to crouch down or stand on tiptoe. To reach the bottom shelves, it can sometimes be easier to work while kneeling! Ergonomics? What's that?

Finally, the shelves of boots are sent for inspection and final packing (Photo 3.3). At this stage of production, the tables are big enough to hold two

PHOTO 3.3 Finishing shelf.

employees. The first inspects the boot and decides to either pass it to the next person for packing, or send it back to the rework department to have its flaws corrected. There are a dozen inspection and packing tables. The inspected and packed product is deposited on a conveyor that takes it to the shipping department, located in another building, by means of an outdoor tunnel.

Experimenting with New Ways of Working

For a period of three months, we try out different ways of producing the duck shoes. Because our employees will now be working standing up and in teams, and this way of working is not the norm in sewing factories, Rita, our industrial engineer, goes looking for potential suppliers for our various needs. Some sewing machines work with more than one pedal—which seamstresses can use simultaneously with two feet—while others oblige workers to use their knee to cut a thread once the seam is finished. From now on, all operations should be done using a single pedal. And we certainly won't be making a standing person crouch to use a mechanism with her knee.

So we import pedals from China, Taiwan, Europe, and the United States, and we test them all. Then we leave the final choice to the module's employees.

Around this same time, I travel to Atlanta, Georgia, to attend the annual clothing industry trade show, the Bobbin Show. When I wander the aisles of the immense exhibition hall where hundreds of companies from all over the globe display their new products, I notice some seamstresses demonstrating a system called the Toyota Sewing System (TSS), created by Toyota for its car seat sewing and assembly factories and sold in the United States. Unfortunately, the consulting firm that acquired the rights to present and sell the sewing system only offers it in turnkey format, which would represent an investment of over $1 million in equipment acquisition and installation just for our smallest service! As well, if we opted for the system, we'd have to buy Toyota® brand sewing machines, Toyota tilting tables, Toyota anti-fatigue mats, and so forth! Such an expense is unimaginable for an SME (small and medium enterprise) like us. Also, I can't understand how such a system could be sold in turnkey format when the biggest change that needs to happen in a factory that wants to move into Lean production is culture change. You could spend millions of dollars on equipment without any guarantee that the new factory would work—it's the employees that ensure the success of this kind of project, not the machinery features. In one sense, however, I must admit that it makes me happy to know such a system exists. I feel reassured at the idea that we aren't the only ones to have thought of applying the TPS* philosophy to a factory like ours.

COMPARISON OF THE RESULTS OBTAINED

When I get back from the Atlanta show, we test various options and rearrange the module layout several times before measuring the performance of the various activities (Photo 3.4). After three days, the results we obtain are so

PHOTO 3.4 Pilot module in action.

TABLE 3.1 Comparison of the Two Production Systems

Activity Measured	Traditional Piecework System	Module (Team)	Improvement (Deterioration)
Work in process	2 weeks	4 hours	95%
Rejects	3%	0.24%	92%
Area occupied	420 square feet	300 square feet	40%
Manufacturing lead time	9 days	1 day	90%
Efficiency	115%	85%	(30%)
Machine/employee ratio	1/1	2/1	—
Value of goods in process	$52,000	$2,600	95%

unexpected that we're scared to talk about them. The improvement is almost instantaneous and very evident. Never would I have imagined such success. When I quickly extrapolate, and I extend the numbers to the other services, the figures are unheard of! With Rita and Monique, we start to calculate the economic benefits of a modular system generalized to the entire factory. Still, I am careful to revise all the extrapolations to make them lower, for fear of being ridiculed when I share this with my boss.

Table 3.1 shows the results of the comparison of the two production systems.

In this metamorphosis, the seamstresses have to trade in a specialization that's sterile, but comfortable, for a fertile but difficult versatility. They need time to learn and master the functioning of several machines at once, while they've so far only ever used one. We have to expect a significant drop in their efficiency at the beginning of their learning curve. But that drop is periph-eral, if anything, because at the same time, the module clocks a considerable improvement in productivity.

PRESENTING AN EXPENSE BUDGET TO MANAGEMENT

The executive board customarily meets every last Friday of the month. But considering the excellent results we obtained with the pilot module, I am so keen to share my observations with the board that I call an exceptional meeting in the middle of the month.

At first glance, the task could seem monstrous: convincing the owners of a family SME to invest hundreds of thousands of dollars in a production sys-tem that will upset everything they've known and built for decades. I should be worried and nervous, but instead I'm sure of myself…confident.

The budget is simple. We need to buy the production machinery, lay out the factory by modules, and repaint it before installing new electrical and pneu-matic equipment. As well, we have to invest—this is really an investment and not an expense—in a tailored training program. The Contrecoeur factory, due to the nature of its operations, holds a great advantage over our other factories when it comes to acquiring equipment. For the cost of an injection molding machine in Montreal, the Contrecoeur factory can buy 100 sewing machines.

TABLE 3.2 Results of the Comparative Analysis

Building Costs	
Purchase of machinery and equipment	$300,000
Modifications to existing equipment (pedals, tables, wheels, etc.)	$60,000
Purchase of an automated leather cutting and measuring system	$70,000
Painting of two floors	$20,000
Electrical and pneumatic work on two floors	$60,000
New factory layout (conveyors, moving, etc.)	$30,000
Total Building Costs	$540,000
Training Costs	
Training fees	$290,000
Salaries for employees in training and in directed practice	$570,000
Gross Training Costs	$860,000
Subsidy for on-the-job training program (OTJ) at $2/h/employee	($400,000)
Tax credit (40%)	($184,000)
Net Total of Training Costs	$276,000

But to spend within our means, we opt to buy secondhand machines that are still in perfect condition. By the same token, we decide to have pedals made to our specific needs and to adapt all our existing tables ourselves, which will help us save tens of thousands of dollars.

Table 3.2 provides the numbers we present at the special management meeting.

By basing ourselves on the results we obtained with the module, we can extrapolate the possible savings for all the products manufactured at the factory, which represents

Direct projected savings	
Direct labor savings	$180,000
Indirect labor savings	$240,000
Work in process savings	$110,000
Elimination of the rework department	$80,000
Total Direct Savings	$610,000

To this, we need to add the indirect savings and benefits:

- 75% improvement and reduction in manufacturing lead time
- 80% reduction in losses due to nonquality
- Recuperation of an area of 4,000 square feet in the factory (instead of having to expand)
- Competitive advantages, as the flexibility obtained will allow us to supply 40 customers or produce 40 different styles simultaneously

Armed with data this convincing and the prospect of a return on investment in just over a year, it is very easy for me to get senior management to agree to let me carry out the project. The detailed plan for my future actions, including training, employee involvement in decision making, and the investment in equipment and physical transformation of the factory, is also accepted unanimously. I make sure, nevertheless, to tell the board members about the scope of the project ahead of us and the disastrous consequences that a failure, even a partial one, could bring.

Let the action begin!

Chapter 4

Getting the Employees Involved

OCTOBER 1992

We once again call a meeting for the employees to tell them about our results. This time, no rumors! This second meeting in the community hall doesn't catch them off guard. They are simply impatient to hear about our results. Monique, Rita, and I are especially enthusiastic, even excited, to share this amazing achievement.

WORRIES AND RESISTANCE AMONG THE EMPLOYEES

To my great surprise, the reactions are mitigated. No excitement, and no buy-in upon hearing the impressive figures listed one after the next. I understand right away that the magnitude of the changes to the employees' reference structure prevents them from seeing the benefits of our plan. Still, this new way of working would solidify their jobs for many years to come. We'll be so much more productive and profitable that it will be difficult to meet the demand. But the fear of the unknown is winning out over the excitement of the moment. To reassure employees as quickly as possible, I explain that a broad training program will be put in place, and that it will touch on, among other things:

- Human relations for employees working as a team
- Work measurement
- JIT*
- *Kaizen* and Lean principles
- Total quality

We then clarify that we'll have to proceed step by step, while ensuring that the pace of the transformation is not too quick. We hope, in doing this, to convey our enthusiasm to the gathered workers. Unfortunately, it doesn't work! We are still seeing the same incredulous, worried expressions!

Next comes a question period during which the main concerns expressed are on the following points:

- Teamwork
- Having to work standing up
- Learning the way new machines work
- New method of remuneration
- Abandonment of individual performance bonuses (with the new team-based bonus not being clearly defined)
- Non-reversibility of the process
- Fear of layoffs due to restructuring

With all these apprehensions on the part of the employees, I must be reassuring and assuage their every doubt before leaving the room. Calming their fears about the first three topics is easy enough; I just need to talk to them about patience, new habits, and the learning curve. But for the other points, my task is more difficult. As soon as we start talking about layoffs, salaries, bonuses, and anything else that affects people's wallets, we need to act carefully and, above all, help people feel safe. And my answers surprise more than one person.

To start with, I tell employees about our own fears, as administrators, because every employee concern holds weight with an employer like us. We are very well aware that we're tackling a project that has already cost some companies dearly when they've made the attempt. The failure rate is greater than the success rate when it comes to JIT implementation. I also explain to them that the concept of a team is no more familiar to us than it is to them. In short, while a team is a group of people, a group of people is not necessarily a team. The shift toward working standing up also requires major investments on the part of the employer, both for equipment and for the dip in production during the adaptation period that needs to be compensated for. The learning period for new machines leads to a massive drop in efficiency, meaning an increase in cost price. We're all in the same boat!

While the employees are very attentive, they don't want to hear about our worries as managers. They were expecting responses to their own! In the packed room, you could hear a pin drop...

Next, despite the worries, I insist on being clear about how it's crucial that everyone be on board with the new project. So I continue, specifying that once the system is implemented, there will be no going back. We first need to believe in it, and then we jump in with both feet! But when we're in it, we'll have to learn how to solve problems and surmount obstacles TOGETHER.

As for layoffs, salaries, and bonuses, I can't honestly offer easy answers. In fact, as JIT pioneers in the shoe industry, we'll be experimenting and discovering the best ways to proceed together, and we'll have to adjust.

GUARANTEES AND COMMITMENTS FROM THE COMPANY

That all being said, because we anticipated the employees' fears, Monique and I have already agreed on a few guarantees we can offer and promises we can make. So this is the right time to share them with our employees. After admitting to them that we don't have the answers to all their questions, I share our intentions with them:

- Employees will not lose a single cent in the transition.
- There will be no layoffs.
- We will train them appropriately on-site.
- To ease the transition to teamwork, we'll offer training on human relations.
- We'll work together to find the best bonus system.
- We'll make the effort to listen to the employees, and we'll coach them throughout the conversion process.
- Employees will take part in all future decisions.
- We'll be much more productive.

After a few murmurs in the room, I can hear sighs of relief, and I even see a few smiles!

*****

I'll make a little aside here to tell you about a funny incident that shows how important it is for each concept to be fully understood by everyone. As soon as the meeting is over, while I'm gathering my documents, one of our good seamstresses, in her 50s, approaches Monique and me timidly. She seems hesitant to tell us something. When I raise my head, I smile and ask if she enjoyed the meeting. She takes a deep breath and says, "I have no problem trying your new system. But what happens in my bedroom between me and my husband is nobody else's business." I wonder what on earth she's talking about, and I look at Monique in bewilderment. The seamstress tries again: "What I mean is that I don't like the idea of having to discuss my 'human relations' with the other employees on my team." Still perplexed, I hear Monique answering her, "Oh my goodness! We said we'd give you classes on human relations, not on sexual relations!" Finally, I get it! After having a good laugh with the employee, we explain the content of human relations classes.

*****

When we come out of the meeting, I look at Monique. She seems even more worried than she was before the meeting. She really understands the height of the mountain we have to climb. A mountain that will take a good three years to scale. Goodbye, 40-hour workweek, weekends, and golf! We're both very aware of the resistance to change that we'll have to surmount. And when it comes to change, we're proposing quite a big one! It's really more like turning things completely upside down. So we're in agreement to proceed in a progressive, rational way with as much transparency as possible.

Chapter 5

New Layout and Training

NOVEMBER 1992

We plan the changes to make to the factory, and we decide to stop all production activities for a period of three months, from December 1992 to February 1993.

PLANNING AND IMPLEMENTING THE NEW LAYOUT

During the renovation period, the factory is transformed into a huge construction site. Maybe more like a battlefield. Not one piece of equipment—machines, conveyors, shelves—comes back to its original place in the new facility. Our traditional factory layout is converted into a modular-type layout; each module contains all the machines needed to manufacture a boot from A to Z. They'll be adapted for versatile employees who'll be working standing up and in teams.

   With the help of Rita, our industrial engineer, and Francis Slater, our head mechanic, we design a standard ergonomic base that serves as a model for the hundreds of new production machines. The bases are equipped with wheels to facilitate equipment transportation within and outside the module; in fact, to manufacture different boot models, we need different machines. And as our new system aims to be as flexible as possible, our objective is to be able to adapt the layout quickly—in less than three minutes—depending on the number of models to produce. The change will be made by the seamstresses who are working in the modules. The wheels mounted on the new bases solve the mobility problem. That said, we are still stuck with the problem of hooking up compressed air and electricity. We can't really consider calling on a mechanic to unplug or replug the equipment every time. After a few tests and evaluations of different methods, we decide to standardize the air supply by

PHOTO 5.1 We remove the windows to bring in the biggest pieces of equipment.

installing quick connectors, and to equip ourselves with an electrical power and distribution system on overhead rails. This way, a seamstress can plug or unplug the air supply and electricity for a machine simply by giving a half-turn to the connection (with a quick-connect type of plug).

To install the largest pieces of equipment, such as the cutting presses near the sewing machines, we're obliged to demolish a few of the building's outside walls (see Photo 5.1). This way, we can place the machinery in the sequence of operations. This configuration is known as "group technology*."

Once the factory is transformed and the new process merger layout is in place, teams of five to eight employees will work in U-shaped modules and will be able to make all the products that Genfoot manufactures.

As shown on the layout plan in Figure 5.1, these modules are placed on both sides of the old conveyor, which was modified to carry only finished, ticketed, and packaged products to the warehouse, where they'll be loaded onto trucks.

The factory is subdivided into three self-sufficient units—leather, nylon, and sport boots—on the two upper floors.

As well, we take the opportunity to repaint the factory from top to bottom. The second and third floors, formerly used for cutting and warehousing, will now sport new colors, creating a more pleasant work environment (see Photo 5.2).

Each of the three units has all the equipment needed for product manufacturing, including dies presses, sewing machines, and more. No more useless moving around to borrow this or that from another section.

All the machines are placed in process convergence to facilitate pull production*. Added-value activities occupy more than 50% of the space.

Production
Services

FIGURE 5.1 New modular layout.

Table 5.1 presents the surfaces occupied before and after the transformations. Figure 5.2 shows a visual of how noticeable the improvements are.

TAILORED TRAINING PROGRAMS

During the renovations, our employees are paid to "go to school." In reality, it's as if school were coming to them, at the factory.

Our training plan affects all our employees, regardless of what they do. In total, 250 people receive tailored training. In the factory and in our warehouse, we set up small classrooms, each grouping together some 20 employees.

PHOTO 5.2 Second floor, freshly repainted.

TABLE 5.1 Traditional Layout versus Modular Layout

	Traditional		Modular	
	(sq. ft.)	(%)	(sq. ft.)	(%)
Production surface	12,500	32.1	16,800	43.0
Stock of raw materials	11,600	29.7	7,000	17.9
Work in process	5,900	15.1	2,300	5.9
Hallways/alleys	5,500	14.1	5,800	14.9
Offices/cafeteria	3,500	9.0	3,300	8.5
Rest area	—	—	500	1.3
Available space	—	—	3,300	8.5
Total	39,000	100	39,000	100

We make sure to lighten the theory classes because most of our employees haven't been to school in 20, 30, or, in some cases, 40 years. For some of them, spending a whole day listening to a teacher drone on about theory is neither stimulating nor interesting. So all the theory classes include group games and role-play scenarios to make them more interactive and fun.

We group jobs together and develop three training plans:

1. For seamstresses: 240 hours per employee, including theory (management and technical) and directed practice
2. For cutters: 220 hours per employee, with theory representing 95% of the training
3. For supervisors: 80 hours of theory training each, plus the 240 hours of training given to the seamstresses

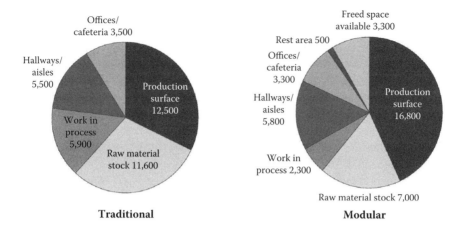

FIGURE 5.2 Comparison of the space used by traditional layout and by modular layout (in square feet).

Seamstresses

The text that follows presents a brief look at the topics addressed in the theory section of the seamstress training.

Human Relations and Communication

This training segment aims to ensure smooth team function. We need to harmonize our seamstresses' module-based work and increase their efficiency. The multidisciplinary teams must be able to produce quality boots and make decisions about how to do assembly or manage rotation within the module, for example, without a manager's intervention.

We place the emphasis on the importance of teamwork. Each person must fully understand and assimilate certain key concepts, such as "a team is as strong as its weakest link," and "a team's strength is greater than the sum of the individual strengths that make it up."

We also address topics such as interpersonal skills, problem-solving techniques, the importance of strong communication, and the encouragement of each person's participation. This training segment is the program's cornerstone. As such, we insist on investing all the time and money we need to make sure our seamstresses master it.

Management

With this block of classes, we want our employees to understand how their production standards are calculated. We set out the industrial engineering principles of work measurement and study, and recall the importance of ergonomics in the design of a work center (module) as well as that of work safety. The seamstresses also learn about calculating cost price and the effect of a reduced volume of work in process on administrative expenses. A good part of the classes is devoted to JIT* principles and the benefits of the TPS*. A little production line simulation illustrates the advantages of module-based work. The teacher explains the way the "hand-to-hand" principle works using a paper boat assembly model. He compares the traditional method to module-based assembly by measuring various activities, to convince the employees of the new method's advantages. Then we come to *Kaizen* principles—the philosophy that emphasizes continued improvement: "Never be satisfied with the status quo, and continually question our work habits" is the concept that closes this first part of the training.

The final section in this block is devoted to quality assurance. We explain the difference between assurance and control when it comes to quality, and we introduce Total Quality Management* (TQM) principles. We teach them how to take responsibility for quality. The program briefly covers some statistics and probability concepts using dice games. Finally, the employees learn to read, evaluate, and write quality reports.

Technical Training

The objective of this training segment is to teach employees how to use the various machines, and to maintain and repair their equipment themselves. We allot a total of 40 hours per employee.

We start by teaching them how their machines work: the components and their placement, the sequence of their movements, and the appropriate safety rules. We also touch on basic calibrations: length and tension point for sewing, machine adjustments, and needle setup. Finally, we explain how to diagnose a problem and repair a broken machine. In sum, we no longer want our seamstresses to call on a mechanic to repair their machines and get them working again. By the end of this theoretical and practical training, they'll be able to do it themselves.

Directed Practice

This training segment aims to ensure a harmonious and productive kickoff starting on the first days of modular production, and to avoid generalized chaos. During their practice, the seamstresses learn to work various machines they've never ever touched. They also get used to stand-up sewing and working in teams. Over the coming weeks, each employee's progress is evaluated using a grid that indicates the machines and skills they've mastered. The supervisors update the grid every day.

To see the improvement every week, it's clear that the time spent in directed practice is inversely proportional to the length of the learning curve. So we invest as much time as possible in coaching our employees and helping them learn the new machines to minimize their learning time. After four weeks, we decide that it will take about three years for the seamstresses to reach the efficiency that we had in the traditional system. But the work pays off vastly, considering the productivity gain in the end.

Cutters

Our cutters are trained to understand leather in depth so they can optimize their use of it. In our traditional system, they were paid only for the total quantity of pieces cut; we weren't counting the quantity of leather used. But leather is the most expensive raw material in boot manufacturing.

First, we teach cutters about the origin and processing of raw skins through to their transformation into leather, the various methods of vegetable and chrome tanning that render them rot-proof; the various parts that make up a skin such as the butt, the shoulder, and the belly; and the characteristics of leather. The cutters also learn to discern the stretch direction of a skin.

I am pleasantly surprised to see the cutters' enthusiasm for their training. Some of them have been cutting leather for more than 20 years without knowing that a skin has a stretch direction. Just watching their reactions, I'm convinced that we'll get a much better product in the future!

We also take the opportunity afforded by the training to introduce a new computerized system designed to optimize the use of leather. The system rewards the good cutters who succeed in saving on leather while respecting their standard time. The bonuses given to them represent 20% of the cost of the leather they've saved. In short, the cutters are encouraged to work using their judgment rather than strictly aiming for fast execution (see Photo 5.3). Once again, goodbye piecework performance bonus, hello intelligent work!

PHOTO 5.3 Cutters working at their cutting presses.

Supervisors

The transition to the new production system makes for a colossal challenge for our supervisors because they have to adapt to a philosophy that drastically transforms their role. Instead of supervisors, they become coaches or trainers. We make sure they understand the importance of their new role and the impact it has on the success of teamwork.

As well as taking part in 240 hours of seamstress training, the supervisors take 80 hours of training specific to them. This more theoretical training supplement focuses on the following subjects:

- The supervisor's role in a JIT environment
- Information systems:
  - Costs
  - Planning
  - Payroll
  - Scheduling
- Total quality:
  - Definition and principles
  - Statistical process control (SPC)
  - Quality audits
  - Their empowerment
  - Their new role in a total quality environment
- Workplace health and safety
- JIT and modular production:
  - The principles of push* and pull production*
  - TPS, *kanbans*, and *Kaizen*
  - Various motivation plans in a teamwork context

Chapter 6

Reviewing the Salary, Structure, and Bonus System

MARCH 1993

The pre-transition salary structure at Genfoot is more complex than our production system! As well, individual bonuses are no longer appropriate in a just-in-time (JIT) and teamwork-based context. So there's cleanup to be done here, too.

A COMPLEX EXISTING SITUATION

The remuneration rates vary based on several criteria, including the models of sewing machine the seamstresses use and the types of materials with which they work. In total, there are 17 different rates based on the tasks being carried out: six for sewing, three for cutting, four for handling, three for finishing and packaging, and one for inspection.

- Sewing:
  - General leather sewing
  - General nylon sewing
  - Felt sewing
  - Sewing on the Puritan® (a three-needle machine that joins bottoms to leather uppers)
  - Sewing with a Pfaff 335 (station where bottoms are sewn to nylon uppers)
  - Sewing with a Mauzer® (a machine used for sewing felt liners)

- Cutting:
  - Leather cutting
  - Nylon cutting
  - Felt cutting
- Materials handling and moving:
  - Stocking workstations with pieces and materials
  - Handling
  - Merchandise shipping and receiving
  - Putting away and fetching felt in the factory
- Finishing and packaging:
  - Waterproofing
  - Packaging
  - Finishing
  - Inspection

In addition, we give a bonus for leather work, but not for nylon or felt work. The bonus is justified by the difficulty of handling leather uppers.

For sewing, the gap between the lowest and highest of the six rates is 14%. It's true that an operation's complexity depends on the materials being assembled (leather-leather, nylon-rubber, and so forth). But in the new system, all the seamstresses will become versatile and work on different machines, taking turns on an equal basis. As well, in a modular manufacturing context, they will only spend 15% of their time sewing, compared to 85% operating machines for which the rates used until now are lower. It seems to go without saying that we should establish a single rate for sewing for the future.

But then, what do we do with the existing rates?

A CRUCIAL SIMPLIFICATION

The situation is not a simple one.

First, I want to keep the promise I made at the general assembly: no employee must lose a penny in the transition. Next, I don't want to penalize the seamstresses who are currently the best paid, and who, generally speaking, are the ones with the most seniority.

After a few meetings with the plant manager and the industrial engineer, we opt for a single base rate for all sewing operations that's somewhere between the current lowest and highest rates. That said, the seamstresses whose rate is currently higher than this single rate will receive a subsidy for a certain time to compensate for their lack of earnings; by our forecasts, the supplement should disappear progressively in four years at most. In a sense, I see it as a reward for the most senior employees who were working on the most complex machines, or as a token of appreciation for services rendered.

Now we just need to determine the base rate for all the seamstresses. This is a critical decision that will influence our cost price but, above all, the salaries of 80% of our employees. So the rate must be both fair and competitive.

Too high and it will damage us in the long run; too low and it will create employee animosity and discontent with change. As we're counting heavily on their motivation to succeed with our project, and because this is, of course, the most important point in their view, we need to weigh our decision carefully. The employees are ready to make big sacrifices, to give us the benefit of the doubt, and trust us, but any change that affects their wallets must be based on very convincing arguments!

In the same vein, with the introduction of a new cutting optimization system, we decide to keep a single rate for all the cutters.

As for inspection and finishing, they'll now be done in the modules by the seamstresses and packagers.

The various handling operations will be grouped into a single handling category, for which a single rate will be set.

In a flash, we've just reduced our number of rates from seventeen to four! To be sure that we avoid making major mistakes that will come back to haunt us later, I consult some data from the Shoe Manufacturers' Association of Canada, which produces a report or database each year listing salaries and benefits paid by its members. Because we ourselves are one of the industry's major employers, we know that our salary rates for seamstresses have been competitive up to this point, but I want to make sure they'll stay that way when we change our pay calculation method. When I see the latest Association numbers, I'm reassured: the rates I discussed with Monique are fair, equitable, and competitive.

SEEKING CONSENSUS

We decide to call a meeting for our factory employee/employer committee to debate the salary rate for sewing (the rates for the other tasks being already set) so that we can reach an agreement. I know that the employees' participation in this decision is a double-edged sword. If greedy employees are unsatisfied with a rate that falls below their expectations, they may block the discussion process. But if we put our cards on the table and reach consensus, it'll work out well!

So we explain to the committee the principle of choosing a single rate for seamstresses, and the way subsidies will work for those who have been making more than the base rate we've used up to this point. When we ask the committee's employee members for their opinion, their answer is unanimous: "It depends on the base rate you choose!" No surprise. I explain that they themselves must choose the rate, but that it must be justifiable and competitive. I add that management has arrived at a number that I'll keep secret until they tell me theirs. The only other comment I make is to ask them to be reasonable in their demands. To help them compare their situation to that of our industry as a whole, we give them the Shoe Manufacturers' Association of Canada report. The employees are pretty uncomfortable with this whole process. This is the first time they're helping make a decision, and they need to be guided a bit. One of the seamstresses looks at me, incredulously, and says, "Are you asking us to decide on our own salary?" Her tone tells me she probably wanted to be saying, "Have you lost your mind?" I improvise by explaining to the employees that, to be popular in the factory, I could level all the seamstresses' salaries upward but that in doing so we'd surely lose our competitive edge. I add offhandedly that, of course, it wouldn't be my problem anymore because my boss would already have fired me! This response seems to relax the committee members. And so begins a good hour-long discussion about the various rates offered elsewhere.

When the employees reach consensus about the hourly wage they want for seamstresses, the rate is $0.20 below ours. When we reveal our number and confirm that we'll hold to it, big smiles appear on their faces. They just proved to us that we can count on their good judgment, and now I know our project is on the right track.

Organizing the Work

JUNE 1993

We now have to tackle work organization. We need to take into consideration quite a number of elements, even if we already have a good idea of how several aspects of our operation will work. What are the advantages and disadvantages of individual work and teamwork? If we opt for teams, how do we make them up? How do we develop autonomy within the modules? Do we still need the inspector position within the new system? These are multiple-choice questions, and we want to get some clearer answers.

INDIVIDUAL WORK VERSUS TEAMWORK

As I mentioned earlier, we are biased toward teamwork. However, we think it's important to conduct a comparative examination of specialized individual work and versatile teamwork. Upon reflection, we list the advantages and disadvantages of each approach, both for employees and for the company management. Our observations are shown in Tables 7.1 and 7.2. Other major advantages of teamwork that both management and employees enjoy include increased loyalty and stronger commitment to ensuring the company's success.

I've said it before: I'm totally against piecework, particularly because employees usually focus on the quantity to produce, to the detriment of product quality, but not only for that reason. My biggest objection to the practice is about employees' self-esteem. When you watch an employee doing piecework, it's like watching a robot at work. A robot needs no judgment: it takes the same pieces from the same containers, places them against the same pattern, and assembles them in the same way. This is the parallel I make when I see an operator doing piecework to install eyelets on a boot. I can't see much

TABLE 7.1 Advantages and Disadvantages of Individual Work

	Advantages	Disadvantages
Management	Employee specialization	Individualism encouraged
	High efficiency or performance	Loss of quality due to work segmentation
Employees	Better control of remuneration	Increased risk of accident due to the fast pace of execution and repetitive movements
	No involvement in other people's problems	
		Isolation

TABLE 7.2 Advantages and Disadvantages of Teamwork

	Advantages	Disadvantages
Management	Versatile labor force	Longer learning time
	Improved quality of finished products	More expensive training
	Increased productivity	Team harmony difficult to achieve
Employees	More satisfying work	Learning of teamwork
	Boost in self-esteem	Need to work standing up
	Feeling of belonging	Proximity of others and need to deal with their failings
	Increased motivation, thanks to satisfaction with the quality of finished products	Need to respect others' work rhythm

difference between her work and the work an automaton would do in her place. To me, this is an insult to the employee's intelligence. The only interest she might find in this way of working is the lure of money.

Yet, even today, thousands of manufacturing companies around the world use piecework as a remuneration model. Even worse, the workers themselves are afraid to see the system disappear. Have you ever heard an employee or union ask that piecework performance bonuses be abolished? It rarely happens.

*****

This reminds me of a story. When I worked with Electrolux®, one day I was sitting at the negotiation table, with a view to renewing a collective agreement. A union representative, frustrated at not being able to exceed the 130% performance cap and the attached remuneration, demanded that piecework be abolished as long as employees were paid by the hour based on their average salary of the preceding year. Because 95% of the employees were reaching 130% performance, the company would have had to pay 130% of the base salary without being able to ask more than the old 100% standard. Completely unreasonable! If there's one good thing about piecework, it's that it requires of the employees a certain level of rigor. They know that if they waste time chatting or taking extended breaks, they won't achieve their optimal performance.

What if employees are happy to do piecework, and the bosses are satisfied with their performance? Why change things? Even when a transformation will improve quality of life, every human being fears change and tends to resist it when it's imposed. And really, some employees do prefer the status quo; they are very happy to not have to make decisions and they simply don't want to take on more responsibility (a number of them told me this explicitly!). So we need to use solid arguments to convince them to move toward new practices. And sometimes, to arrive at our goal, we need to be a little daring, even if it upsets some.

CAREFULLY CONSIDERED TEAM COMPOSITION

I entrust work team composition to Monique, the plant manager. She's the best-placed person to make a judicious choice. She knows every employee's name, their experience, their personalities, and their potential.

We see several options for team formation:

1. Grouping together the experienced seamstresses so that less skilled ones don't hold them back.
2. Combining "old hands" (an in-house expression to refer to the older seamstresses, meaning the most experienced) and younger ones, so that the latter inherit the tricks of the trade.
3. Grouping together seamstresses of the same height in a module so that machine heights can be adjusted for optimal ergonomics.
4. Associating employees by affinity (placing friends together, for instance) to encourage harmony and team spirit in the modules.

After discussing it, we go with the second option while taking into account the leadership and communication abilities of the more experienced people. Because she knows her employees well, Monique makes sure to separate strong personalities to head off confrontations within the teams. Nevertheless, for ergonomic reasons, we create three special modules for employees of exceptional heights: one for the very tall ones (5' 7" and up) and two for the very short ones (under 5' 2"). For the others, whose height varies within four inches or so, the workstation's ergonomic impact will be much less significant: even if some stations are not perfectly tailored to their height, with rotation the seamstresses won't spend more than 20 seconds at a time in one spot.

DEVELOPING AUTONOMY

From piecework to teamwork, there's quite a gulf, and employees can't jump it easily. Our efforts to get there are all the more dispiriting as we only have rare examples to go by. In fact, none of the books I read that discuss multi-disciplinary teamwork in a just-in-time* (JIT) context mention problems like the ones we're facing—even in passing. Quite the opposite—the authors sing the praises of self-managed work teams and their positive impacts on the company and its employees as though it all worked well straight out of the gate. We're nevertheless aware of the challenge we must carry out on this point. This is why we devote significant time to human relations and teamwork in the classes described in Chapter 6 (you may have noticed).

In our case, we have to admit that, at first, confusion reigns in the modules. The employees take several weeks to assume their new responsibilities. We accept this during the in-between period because we don't want to impose a work method on the newly formed groups, nor do we want to force them to choose a team leader. We instead let them decide on their internal work method.

Our wait is rewarded because shortly after, they really impress us with the originality and diversity of their solutions. Some prefer team leaders who change every day or every week. Others name spokespersons to represent them to management. The most original module designates an "engineer" for production standards, an "accountant" for salary-related problems, a "quality supervisor" in liaison with the quality assurance director, a "human resources specialist" to handle conflicts within the team, and a "supplier" to ensure the delivery of the components necessary for JIT production. A few teams even give themselves names, such as "the Gazelles" or "the Old Hands," and so forth.

The way to rotate team members through the various workstations is also left up to the modules. Even if we want a hand-to-hand (also called pair-to-pair) process to facilitate pull production, we let the teams figure out its worth on their own. We only insist on the importance of rotation in the modules because it's crucial that the employees don't lose what they learned on the various machines during their weeks of directed practice training. Some teams decide to rotate every hour. Others prefer to wait for their breaks to change places—breaks that happen four times a day. A small number of teams practice a hand-to-hand process that forces them to change machines every minute, or nearly. The learning takes longer, and the efficiency is lower than expected.

One of the greatest challenges faced by every company that wants to implement autonomous teams is to motivate the operators to change their work habits and make decisions. We are forced to observe that in many cases, they're not ready to or interested in taking on all-purpose manager responsibilities! Even if they received ad hoc training for this purpose, we have to be aware that we're asking them to become more autonomous and creative overnight, as well as continually seeking to improve. And in reality, how many of them have the ambition, education, or personality to exercise the type of leadership we're seeking?

The reality in our factory is that less than 40% of our employees have completed their high school education. Among these undereducated people, many no doubt felt safe in their simple and repetitive tasks. Even with training, do they have the desire and capacity to function in such an environment?

The solution isn't simple or evident. Without losing sight of our goal, we try to respect the employees' choices. We count on the emergence of natural leaders in each team to coordinate the work and assume additional responsibilities. But we also need to face the fact that the employees less inclined toward autonomy and more accustomed toward a certain routine will simply follow the flow. We can't force them to change, at the risk of creating health problems such as stress or professional burnout!

A FACTORY WITHOUT INSPECTORS: IS IT POSSIBLE?

In a restructuring like ours, inspector positions are no longer required because the employees have received the training they need to do their own inspection. The responsibility for quality is transferred to the employees working in production. For example, during manufacturing, the seamstresses themselves carry out the inspection. Then, the packers ensure that the ticketing and packaging meet customer specifications. The customers, more and more demanding, are transferring to us many ticketing operations that used to be carried out in stores. And each customer has its own requirements: for some, the price must be attached to the first ring on the left foot; for others, the third eyelet on the right foot, and so forth. To eliminate packaging errors, we equip each module with a book indicating every customer's specifications.

As for our ex-inspectors, all except one are reassigned to other tasks in the factory. We keep only one inspection position for carrying out quality control on products in-house. The inspector, stationed at the end of the finished product conveyor, conducts planned random control. She goes over selected boxes with a fine-toothed comb to ensure that the products they contain comply with the specification book. From the thread color to the thickness of the leather or nylon, everything is checked. In short, the inspector is the customer's eye—or, should I say, magnifying glass—in our factory. Her task is equivalent to carrying out a product audit before delivery. The inspector reports all anomalies, even the tiniest ones, to the supervisor of the relevant department. The supervisor comes by to see the situation directly. As needed, he returns the box to the module, where immediate corrective action is taken. If the anomaly happens above a certain frequency, it's interpreted as systematic, and a general inspection and process correction ensue.

Given the scope of the change that we've undertaken, the "quality guardian" position held by the inspector helps me sleep better at night! That said, at the moment, my medium-term objective is to eliminate the position.

PUTTING IT TO THE TEST

Every year we get a visit from our major customers' quality inspectors. These inspectors generally spend a day in each of our factories to conduct their own quality audits. They verify our procedures and our quality files, and in some cases they give us a sort of report card, with grades.

After we start our transition, one of our main American customers announces that its inspector will be visiting our Contrecoeur factory. The auditor has heard about our new system and is looking forward to seeing it in action. Accompanied by our quality assurance director, he takes a day to observe, analyze, and verify all the operations carried out on his customer's products. I can tell right away that he likes what he sees. As well, he says that we have the most productive shoe factory he's ever toured in North America. We're impatient to see the grade he gives us before he leaves.

I know he's never given a supplier a grade above 78% in his 12 years as an auditor, but his attitude and comments suggest that things could be different this time. Imagine my disappointment when we get a grade of 81%! If the most productive factory in North America can't do better than that, the industry as a whole must be pretty pathetic!

I want to know where we lost so many points, to improve our performance before his next visit, so I ask the auditor some questions. To my shock, we lost 10 points because our ratio of inspectors to production employees is much lower than the customer's standard of 1 to 20. Come on! He can't be serious, I tell myself! I can't create 15 inspector jobs that I would have to pay to carry out work already done by other employees! That would be utter nonsense.

So we explain to the auditor that all the production employees are trained to conduct inspections and write noncompliance reports within their modules; we have no trouble convincing him that our procedure is a good one. Unfortunately, he explains, he's not the one who wrote the rules; he just applies them. Apologizing that he can't change our grade, he promises that he'll discuss the problem with his superiors. I politely let him know that he can invite his bosses to visit us anytime they wish.

The next year, the customer abolishes the inspector/employee ratio of 1 to 20, and we get a grade of 91%.

That said, on our end, we realize that the quality auditing work done by our single inspector is indispensable. Years after our new system is in place, the quality guardian position still exists, and I have no intention of eliminating it!

KICKOFF PROBLEMS AND FRICTION

We had anticipated some resistance from the employees in regard to organizational change, but not the scope of human problems we are facing. These first difficulties don't take long to surface.

Health Problems

Working standing up causes fatigue issues for the seamstresses. They complain of backaches, tendonitis, bursitis, varicose veins, pain in their shoulders, elbows, hands, legs, and plenty more. These health problems cause many medical absences. It goes without saying that the cost of the factory's premiums to the Commission de la Santé et de la Sécurité du Travail (CSST) explodes.

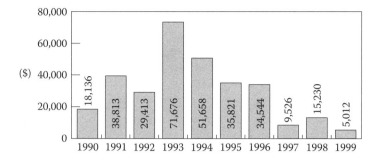

FIGURE 7.1 CSST premiums for the years 1990 to 1999.

In Quebec, the CSST is the government organization that manages the financial end of workplace accident compensation. The CSST calculates a premium rate for each company based on its performance and its area of activity, and then applies that rate to the payroll base. The bigger the company, the higher the portion of the compensation it assumes. As such, the employer covers CSST at 1.2 to 4.4 times the costs linked to a workplace accident, based on the unit rate (meaning the manufacturing sector). For example, for an injury that results in costs of $50,000, the CSST can bill up to $220,000 to the employer.

As shown in Figure 7.1, the implementation of JIT at the Contrecoeur factory caused a 144% increase in compensation costs between 1992 and 1993.

We are very aware that working standing up is becoming more and more tiring, and that we need to solve the issue of workstation ergonomics. While rotation mitigates the problem, it doesn't solve it.

A fact worth noting, however: after this, the number of accidents and injuries drops, leading to a significant reduction in the company's premium rate, to the point that in 1999, the rate is 2.56 while the footwear industry rate as a whole is 4.34. Figure 7.2 illustrates this drop. In the coming chapters we'll discuss how we achieve this.

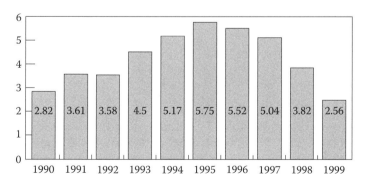

FIGURE 7.2 CSST premium rate for the years 1990 to 1999 (in $ per $100 of payroll).

Tensions within the Teams

The problems in our modules are not only related to health. In fact, they're also—and above all—due to internal rivalries.

In some teams, the tension is so intense that it almost results in fighting. A number of crises occur, and seamstresses at the end of their patience are ready to come to blows. To reduce friction, some modules decide to drop the team leader role because it seems that the ones elected to it are behaving like bosses. In addition to the spiking number of workplace accidents—real or fake ones*—the tension in the modules is at an unsustainable high, and life at the factory becomes very unpleasant. In short, no joke, I can tell you we're on the verge of disaster!

The contrast is particularly striking for me because the factory had always impressed me with its family-like feel. Everyone seemed jovial and good humored, when taken individually. (Yet it must be said that even if they were smiling, the employees were chiefly concerned with their own production or their own operations.) It always seemed to me that if you take a number of happy employees and put them together in a team, that should make for even greater "collective" happiness. Unfortunately, that's not what happens.

Of course, the problem seems even more serious in a small town like Contrecoeur, where the employees all know one another. Because they go to the same stores, restaurants, churches, and so forth, all the problems they have at the factory bleed outside it too.

As I've said, in all the books and the hundred-some articles I've read about the Toyota Production System* (TPS) and autonomous teamwork, I've never seen a single word on the difficulties we're dealing with! None of these texts address the problem of the sharp tensions that we're seeing in some of our teams. They only discuss the benefits and advantages of self-managed teams. In their world, everything seems pretty and perfect. The employees adore the concept, and the employer reaps only benefits. Not so much here! Are we so different from everyone else?

Regardless, we absolutely must create an environment where our employees can rediscover the pleasure of working in harmony and safety. But how?

On a more positive note, at least: the few modules that practice hand-to-hand gradually step up their pace, and harmony seems to reign.

Frustrations about the Removal of Privileges

During one of my tours of the *gemba**, I notice a crowd of seamstresses in the nylon section. It really doesn't look like a work meeting or a *Kaizen** project. They're talking and yelling so loudly that the other teams have stopped working to watch the argument. In response to our questions, they explain to the

---

* Unfortunately, some employees (luckily they are a minority) use any change to their work as an excuse to fake a working accident. They get paid 90% of their salary to stay home.

manager and me that the tension between some teammates is such that they're ready to fight. Monique calms everyone down and asks them to start work again. Wanting to do the right thing, I politely ask one of the two about the reason for their conflict. Instead of answering, she gives me a piece of her mind, saying that we, the management, are paid to make decisions and lead, and that she is quite simply unable and uninterested in taking on responsibilities in an autonomous team! Without letting me get a word in edgewise, she lashes out and takes out her anger on me.

"It's since you showed up here that our problems started," she says. "We were doing fine before all the changes you're making!" The dam has broken, so she continues: "Since you showed up, we've lost all our rights, and…"

I decide to interrupt her because at this rate, soon she'll be blaming me for the fact that it's raining today! "Whoa! Just a minute, please! What rights are you talking about?"

"The right to smoke, drink, and eat at our workstations," she shoots back with vehemence. "The right to leave our spots as needed (read: leaving the factory to deposit our checks at the bank across the street or buying groceries during work hours). You even drew yellow lines on the floor to keep us in place. We feel like prisoners here!"

Now, I can't help but smile, and I breathe a little easier. She's not talking about rights, but about certain unacceptable privileges that were common in the factory before my arrival. Calmly, I take advantage of the crowd to convey a few key messages.

"All the things you just listed out at top speed," I say, "they aren't rights, but privileges that result from lack of discipline. I have no intention of touching your rights. But discipline, on the other hand, yes! It's part of my responsibilities, and my boss pays me to make sure it's respected. And believe me, we have a ways to go. Do you think our customers would like brushing your cigarette ash out of their boots? Or seeing a coffee stain on a beautiful leather or nylon boot? You're confusing rights and privileges. Eating or drinking at your station, those aren't rights. For those things, we've set up break areas in each of your sections. And have you ever thought that maybe you're bothering your coworkers with your cigarette? Have you heard about the dangers of secondhand smoke inhaled by nonsmokers? Consider yourselves lucky that you didn't have me as a workmate, because I'd never have agreed to breathe in your smoke all day. In any case, the law will soon forbid anyone from smoking in public places[*]. But I wouldn't wait for the law if even a single nonsmoker among you complained, because it's my duty to deal with this."

I glance over the little crowd, but nobody argues. Then I lash out in turn, adding, "As for your comment about the yellow lines, I think you're going a bit too far. Those lines set out aisles for circulation. In my whole life, I've never seen a proper factory without them! They protect you from moving dollies. And we can finally see around us clearly!"

---

[*] In Quebec, it's been illegal to smoke in the workplace since 1998.

At that point, a number of them nod their heads in agreement and start to lean toward my side. There are a few giggles here and there, and everyone goes back to their station. As for me, I realize there's still a lot of work ahead!

A CONCESSION TO BENEFIT WORKPLACE ATMOSPHERE

In a piecework environment, every seamstress performs her task solo, without concern for anything else. Here, each of them has a Walkman® and tunes into her favorite station during work hours. This practice has always been tolerated at the factory; so in the employees' view, it's a right they've acquired over the years.

When we moved into modular work, we put an end to this habit, explaining to the seamstresses that with our new manufacturing methods, communication between team members is key. As soon as a problem arises, the whole team has to stop working and discuss possible solutions. How can good communication happen within a team if the seamstresses, plugged into their radios, can't talk to each other?

The decision is quite unpopular; but while there are a few grumbles here and there as we expected, the employees go along with it anyway. Yet I'm well aware that things won't stay like this, and that I'll hear talk of it for years to come. And, in fact, not a single factory committee meeting takes place without the subject coming up. The seamstresses complain about not being able to listen to their music while working. Instead, they have to listen to their teammates' family stories and troubles. In their view, the problems that we had when the modules were launched are now sorted out, and they don't need to communicate nearly as frequently. They say that if they were allowed to listen to their Walkmans and a problem should arise, they'd just have to pull out their headphones, talk and come to a decision, and then start working again.

The idea of a central radio for the whole factory doesn't appeal to anyone on the committee.

Monique and I listen carefully to their complaints but we're not ready to concede anything at this stage because we still have issues to deal with when it comes to team operations. We agree with the seamstresses on a few points but insist on assessing things in terms of employee health and safety before reconsidering our decisions.

Because there are no forklifts or other heavy machinery circulating in the factory, there's no risk of serious injury due to collisions, even for an employee who's listening to a Walkman; so we don't need to worry about safety-related dangers. The health risks I see come from the fact that some employees, especially the young ones, bust their eardrums listening to their music so loudly that it bothers their neighbors. (For me personally, their musical choices sometimes stress me out, but it's not my job to impose my taste.)

After some new discussions, the committee members are ready to promise us that efficiency will increase by 10% if we allow them to use Walkmans.

PHOTO 7.1 Employees who are proud of their accomplishment.

They need say no more. Because my office is in Montreal, they don't know that I myself love to listen to the radio at work; there's nothing more relaxing than a little quiet background music.

At this same time, one of our biggest customers announces that he'll be sending his quality director to our factory to audit our ISO 9002* program. If we get certification from our customer, we'll be the first supplier in our area of activity to obtain it. Monique and I inform the employees at the monthly committee meeting and take the opportunity to ask for everyone's collaboration in reaching the goal. The carrot: if we pass the audit on the first try? We promise them that we'll let them use Walkmans at a reasonable volume in the future.

Six weeks later, we welcome the customer's senior managers, who come to award us a plaque for our certification. We organize a big party at the factory to celebrate the achievement and reward our employees. I don't know if they're celebrating because of our certification or because now they can use their Walkmans again, but the point is that in the four weeks that follow, the modules' efficiency jumps by 6% to 13% (see Photo 7.1)!

Chapter 8

Overcoming the Obstacles

NOVEMBER 1993

An unexpected event that could have derailed our organizational transition process ends up putting us on a path to constructive solutions.

A THUNDERCLAP

One fine morning, an inspector from the Commission de la Santé et de la Sécurité du Travail (CSST) (Quebec's workplace health and safety commission) shows up at the company's door. He asks Monique, the manager, for permission to tour the factory. When asked about the nature of his surprise visit, he says he received an anonymous call from an employee reporting the immense "danger" to which employees are exposed by the new practice of sewing in a standing-up position.

After a short tour of the factory, during which he talks with a few module employees and the members of our health and safety committee, he asks to meet the plant manager to share his observations. To her great shock, he reproaches Genfoot for its lack of respect toward its employees because they need to sew standing up. The man is unhinged! He demands that we reinstate the previous conditions, failing which he could stop us from producing! The inspector, who's on the verge of retirement, is clearly not aware of the organizational change we've undertaken. It's also clear that he knows nothing about modular work or stand-up sewing work, and that he doesn't understand the Toyota Lean* system or just in time* (JIT). Monique can only politely get rid of him by strongly suggesting that he ask his superiors about these new operating approaches. As well, given his level of aggression and close-mindedness,

55

she makes it clear that he's no longer welcome in our factory, and she recommends that he retire!

Just after the inspector's visit, Monique hurries to the phone to let me know what just happened. Without wasting a moment, we take steps and contact the CSST head office to report the incident.

The next day, another inspector—a younger one—shows up at the factory. His attitude is totally different from his predecessor's: he's thrilled with what he sees. But while he's there, he makes a very interesting suggestion.

PERFECT TIMING FOR A NEW PROJECT

The new inspector is also a student specializing in ergonomics who's in the last year of his master's degree at the Université du Québec à Montréal (UQÀM). Because our problem is about the rise in workplace accidents, which we need to deal with as quickly as possible, he proposes that we take part in a study led by some ergonomics specialists, including his professor. The team wants to launch a scientific project that will consider musculoskeletal problems in a manufacturing environment. While he can't guarantee that our company will qualify for the project, he promises that he'll submit our application to his professor and his research group.

It turns out that the researchers at UQÀM's Centre d'étude des interactions biologiques entre la santé et l'environnement (CINBIOSE) are very interested in the unique nature of our implementation; but before we can move ahead with the project, it must be approved by the Institut de Recherche Robert-Sauvé en Santé et en Sécurité du Travail (IRSST), a workplace health and safety research institute. On our end, we need to authorize the publication of the study's results, minus identifying details. If it's completed, the project will also be presented at an international conference, PREMUS (the International Scientific Conference on Prevention of Work-Related Musculoskeletal Disorders), which takes place in Montreal in spring 1995.

How could we refuse an opportunity like this? Without delay, we meet with the lead researcher and commit to working with her team for two years with the aim of improving our workstations' ergonomics, but also to reduce the frequency of our accidents.

Our project's official submission to the PREMUS conference, addressed to the IRSST, is accompanied by a cover letter. Here's an excerpt:

> Project title: Obstacles to the implementation of new work organization in a boot factory.
>
> […] However, this new work setup is encountering implementation difficulties. After one year, it has been noted that the planned rotation from one machine to the next within the modules is not being followed. The positions were laid out in a new way so that the seamstresses went from working seated to working standing up. As such, each person can move from machine to machine from one end of the module to the next, producing a complete boot each time. But these

seamstresses have always been specialized in a single type of job or machine, and despite training efforts and financial incentives from the company, they have not acquired this versatility. As well, while some teams have succeeded in exceeding the production goals, the company would like to resolve the tensions that exist within the modules. They are also noting an increase in musculo-skeletal problems resulting from the new methods.

The various steps of constructing a boot often correspond to very physically demanding operations, and a number of WMSD (work-related musculo-skeletal disorder) risk factors can be observed: major wrist deviations, boots held without support, the weight of the rubber-based boots, holding of static positions during the operations, short cycles. The work on some machines can also require a high level of knowledge, without which they may require double the effort. We suspect that musculoskeletal constraints may be at the root of both the implementation difficulties with this new work setup and of the inter-personal tensions within the modules. The strong need for training on certain machines, as well as the difficulties in adapting to the new setup, may also constitute obstacles.

This module-based work setup is new in Québec but seems to be becoming increasingly popular. It provides economic advantages and offers workers the opportunity to increase their skills and engage more fully in the production process, which is often recommended in studies to improve repetitive work conditions. We believe that a study of the 300 people in this factory who have worked within this system for a year represents a great opportunity to better understand the interactions between organizational, social, and biomechanical factors that can contribute to the development of musculoskeletal problems.

Luckily, the project is accepted, and we can move forward.

PRELIMINARY STUDY TO PINPOINT THE PROBLEMS

To carry out the project, we have to create a joint committee formed mostly of production employees along with a few administrators to support the CINBIOSE specialists. Epidemiologists and technicians from McGill University, a sociologist, and representatives of the Montreal public health department also take part. The study involves all the company's employees who worked for at least six weeks in 1994, for a total of 376 people, meaning 98% of the factory's population.

Next, we discuss the methodology we follow in order to evaluate the time and money we'll have to invest in the project.

The joint committee receives training on risk factors, the determinants of musculoskeletal problems, and ergonomic interventions. It follows the study's progress by discussing the results obtained at each step.

At the preparatory step, we develop a short questionnaire (15 to 20 minutes) that is distributed to all employees. It looks at musculoskeletal problems and other work difficulties, and helps draw a portrait of the factory's population, to gather information on people's perception of the changes and their satisfaction level, and to summarize all the difficulties. The results serve to target three or four modules that will be subject to comparative analysis of work activity. The analysis centers on very specific aspects of the work, and on testing hypotheses built on the earlier results. It will also help us to better understand the source of the problems and to make recommendations.

Portrait of the Factory Population

Our joint committee conducts a first analysis, which reveals the following profile for the factory population:

- Sex:
  - 89.6% women
  - 10.4% men
- Average age: 37.2 years
- Seniority:
  - 7.2 years, on average
  - 38.1% have been employees for less than 2 years
  - 33.6% have been employees for more than 10 years
- Education: 38.7% have a high school diploma
- Family income:
  - 26.8% earn less than $20,000
  - 35.6% earn between $20,000 and $40,000
  - 33.1% earn between $40,000 and $60,000
  - 4.4% earn over $60,000
- Status:
  - 74.6% are married
  - 17.2% are single

First Investigation into Health Problems

To begin the study proper, we distribute a first 29-page questionnaire with 91 questions. We set up individual meetings to make sure that the answers are authentic and confidential. At this preliminary stage of the project, the goal is to identify and analyze the various sources of pain and discomfort resulting from the new standing-up work position.

   Some questions are general; for example,

- Are you more stressed out, just as stressed out, or less stressed out than before the changes?
- Are you mentally tired after your workday?
- Are you physically tired after your workday?
- In general, do you experience pain or discomfort?
- Can you circle the parts of your body where you have felt pain or discomfort [on a diagram of the human body]?

Next come questions about the degree of difficulty (less, the same, or more) that the seamstresses perceive in their everyday personal tasks since we implemented the new system at the factory; for example,

- Washing or drying hair
- Placing an object on a high table
- Carrying grocery bags
- Vacuuming
- Opening a sealed food container
- Holding a water pitcher
- Remaining standing or sitting
- Walking or bending over

After reading the questions, the plant manager and I start to seriously question the usefulness and potential results of the questionnaire. It seems to us that everyone will answer: yes, we have pain; yes, we're stressed out; yes, we're tired. We fear that the employees will use these results to force us to review our new production system, which is tiring them, stressing them out, and causing them more trouble than the old system. We're aware that if we continue the process, we won't be able to turn a deaf ear to the problems; so we must be ready to roll up our sleeves, face our responsibilities, and "take the bull by the horns."

But what reassures me is that I have faith in our new philosophy. I am well aware, for instance, that task rotation is not being applied in all the modules, and I hope the study's results will convince the workers to adopt the work method that we think is a good one. If we can clearly demonstrate the direct link between the absence of rotation and the number of work accidents, I'll be satisfied. How many times have we repeated the same speech to employees, only to see them ignore it? Maybe only a third party, such as a consultant, can convince people that it's a well-founded idea. It's very frustrating, but as the proverb says, "nobody's a prophet in their own land."

Second Investigation into Problems with Psychological Well-Being and Communication

A few weeks later, we receive a second questionnaire, 34 pages with 96 questions about teamwork, the satisfaction with the new work method, relationships between employees and supervisors, and so forth.

We expect that the study's results will require us to make some adjustments but it's a risk we're ready to take. Still, the expressions of frustration and distress gathered from our workers shake us up quite a bit, and open our eyes to some problems; we knew they existed, of course, but didn't realize how widespread they were. Judge for yourselves when you read the comments from the first group of 23 workers in three different modules.

- On the subject of working standing up:
  - "Standing up increases the risk of aggravating my neck pain."
  - "With all the time I spend glued to my machine without moving, I'm drained."
  - "We're off balance because of the pedal."
  - "Standing up, we can't have the same productivity; we get tired too quickly."
  - "Even for lacing the shoes and boots, we're not allowed to sit down; we're riveted in place."
- On the subject of communication within the module:
  - "The advantage of the module is that we can communicate, but we don't communicate, so it's as if we were each alone."
  - "The hardest thing is the fights, the personal conflicts."
  - "We never hold meetings to avoid arguments."
  - "We don't dare tell another girl to come help us."
  - "I'm a closed kind of person and I don't say so; I'm blocked, and I can't talk."
- On the subject of personality clashes between employees:
  - "We get criticized."
  - "We get told a bunch of crap; we're all tired."
  - "Some people don't take advice."
  - "There are too many bosses in the module."
  - "Sometimes we don't like someone and she gets on our nerves, but we're forced to deal with her all the time."
- On the subject of the former supervisors' requirements and attitudes:
  - "The 100% standard is sometimes too high."
  - "We feel watched, cut down by the supervisor."
  - "If they don't trust us, we can't trust them."
  - "The supervisor plays favorites."
- On the subject of requirements and attitudes of other workers in the module:
  - "Stress happens when you do your best and the others aren't happy with it."
  - "It makes me angry when others work slower than I do."
  - "I feel watched by another employee."
  - "Yesterday, I took a day off because I was too tired, and I wondered what the other girls in the module would say; I don't feel free."
  - "Some employees push for us to produce more."
- On the subject of having difficulty depending on others' work:
  - "Some are too slow, and that overloads the others."
  - "She said that if things were going badly for her, it was because of my work."
  - "We always have to wait for the slowest ones."
  - "We wait after everyone and everyone waits after us."
  - "It's difficult to depend on others and have others waiting for you."
- On the subject of task distribution:
  - "The others think that in packaging, we don't do anything."

- "I get livid (I am beside myself) when I see girls stopped, chilling out, and doing nothing."
- "Some people do other people's work."
- "We'd all have to work at the same speed, but each task takes a different amount of time; it depends on the model of shoe or boot that we're producing."
- "I don't think it's fair because there's no rotation in the team, and several people are waiting for me but they don't come help me."
- On the subject of help from others/helping others:
  - "The more you help, the less they do."
  - "I always have to tell them to bring me rubber bottoms."
  - "It's as if they don't see what the others are doing."
  - "Some don't want to help out at the stations they're afraid of."
  - "I'm told: you don't know where the work is at, you don't understand when or how to help out your colleagues."
- On the subject of rotation:
  - "Rotation is impossible because I can't work on the machines; I'm too slow."
  - "We could never learn the other tasks because the work has to be cranked out."
  - "The more they want us to produce, the less rotation we do."
  - "Nobody wants to work on my machine. The others are afraid of it."
  - "If I make a mistake at my station, I have to make repairs and everyone has to wait for me."
- On the subject of work conditions that increase difficulties:
  - "When a replacement comes into the team, she throws off our balance."
  - "The boxes are heavy."
  - "We're always getting moved from one module to another."
  - "Over time, handling the big sizes gets heavy (it's tiring because they weigh a lot)."
  - "When someone's missing from a station, it's hard to replace them."
- On the subject of lack of space in the modules:
  - "When I move my boxes, I'm always afraid of hitting someone, or tripping on a pedal or a piece of carpet."
  - "I'm suffocating; we're always tripping over each other."
  - "There's a greater danger of accidents because the module's space is narrow: you can trip on pedals, or jostle a colleague and make her stick herself with a needle."
  - "We're always waiting on someone."
  - "When you don't feel well, you don't feel like getting jostled."
- On the subject of the pace of implementation and insufficient training:
  - "The change happened too quickly."
  - "Many of us didn't get the six weeks of training to learn all the machines."
  - "It takes six to eight months at least to get comfortable on my machine."
  - "On my machine, it takes a year of training to reach my work speed."

- "I didn't learn all the machines when I was trained."
- On the subject of nostalgia for the old system:
  - "Before, we could have our own rhythm."
  - "Before, when you didn't feel well, you could slow down; you had your banked coupons."
  - "Before, I was more productive."
  - "Before, we had chairs."
- On the subject of the positive elements of the new system:
  - "It's pretty nice to be able to communicate with one another."
  - "It's interesting to see all the steps of boot manufacturing."
  - "There's no pile-up of mistakes; we know right away if there's a problem with our way of doing something."
  - "I'd like the module system if there was a rotation."
  - "I like the ambiance when things are going well with the girls."
  - "Before, people took things too far: the girls would go off and run errands during work hours."

On the subject of what they like about their work, most of the workers answered that they like sewing and they like their work, their trade. This is a very positive aspect of the situation summary at the point when the study is launched. But to quote one of the women who answered the questionnaire: "Teamwork is a lot of work!"

Summary and a Concrete Plan of Action

Faced once again with major difficulties and negative comments, we could have been discouraged. After all, we've already invested so much in training employees and coaches to prevent this kind of situation. But, as mentioned earlier, we believe in the Lean system and we are ready to overcome the obstacles. We're in this to win! We're convinced that we have to bring out the positive, even in a negative situation. So this is what we decide to do, inspired by the last two groups of employee comments about the positive aspects of the new methods and their love for the work. In summary, while the investigation step is long, difficult, and costly, we believe it has also been very profitable because it helps us make a number of progressive and positive decisions.

In light of the employees' statements, we have to solve two series of problems at the factory: (1) musculoskeletal or ergonomic problems and (2) communication problems within the modules.

Monique and I are convinced that rotation is beneficial but we leave the ergonomics solutions to our on-site specialists; they undertake an in-depth study and eventually develop a plan to put an end to musculoskeletal problems. As for the two of us, we focus instead on the needs for additional training.

I realize that at the stage we've reached, this is no longer a question of a 20- or 40-hour course. We need a training plan that will play out over a much longer period of time, and establish a training and continuing improvement process for each module. It's imperative that we drain the abscess that is impeding the teams' operations. We need to experiment, test, and implement new ways to produce, communicate, and perform.

We don't want to call on an external consultant who'll try to find time to give us a hand between two contracts and then leave to work with another client. We need the continual presence in the factory of a trainer, a facilitator specialized in human relations, an industrial psychologist who can rally the troops—and this person must be available immediately! But we also can't hire this specialist permanently. So the job will have to focus on in-house trainers and coaches to make them good facilitators.

THE FACILITATOR: A POSITIVE AGENT FOR CHANGE

Sometimes, the stars align in funny ways.

Every Friday night, my wife and I play volleyball in a friendly mixed league. After a couple of hours of play, most of the team ends up going out for a coffee and catching up. On one of these nights, I'm chatting with one of them, a mechanical engineer who works for SNC-Lavalin. Jean-Pierre is curious about what's going on at the Contrecoeur factory and always enjoys hearing the latest about the project on which I'm spending all my time. When I talk to him about the team problems, he recommends that I get in touch with his neighbor, who teaches in human resources at the Université de Montréal. He tells me that Pierre-Paul Bilodeau, the neighbor referred to, often talks with him about our work method, which is becoming more and more widespread. Without really knowing whether this professor can help me, he gives me his contact information.

The next morning, I call Pierre-Paul and we decide to meet in Contrecoeur the following Tuesday. I insist on meeting him at the *gemba** with Monique joining us. Our visitor arrives as planned at 10 a.m. and, after standard introductions, we decide to start with a tour of the factory. Pierre-Paul is very distinguished. He's tall, elegant, speaks well, is always smiling, and according to the secretaries, he's a good-looking man. After touring the factory (and turning a few heads), we return to Monique's office. Our visitor is enthralled with what he's just seen.

After a mere 15 minutes of discussion, I'm certain that he'll fit perfectly into our project as a facilitator. He gives me the impression that he's the perfect confidant, the go-to guy you would talk to anytime you had a problem. He knows his stuff, he's very patient, and above all, he's a good listener! He understands the principle of work teams in depth, and has even published books on the subject. Only his lack of practical experience makes me hesitate to offer him the job. But how many specialists can boast practical facilitation experience in a sewing factory? Also, Pierre-Paul wants to work in the private sector and apply all the concepts he's been teaching all these years. He's at a crossroads, and he is hesitating to renew his contract as a professor because he wants to move on to new things. When I present him our proposal, his eyes light up. This is his dream opportunity to apply his knowledge! He's also very flexible in terms of schedule. We agree on an 18-month term, give or take four months. Depending on how the project evolves and what progress is made, we could shorten or lengthen his term by a few months. It's a match made in heaven, promising a sure success!

Following our agreement, Pierre-Paul submits a hands-on, customized training plan to us. He also consults with our team of musculoskeletal specialists. A few days later, he proposes a program focused on the factors that foster healthy module and work team management. Here are the key points:

   I. Rethinking management's leadership
      Clarifying expectations and scope of responsibilities
  II. Working to acquire essential skills
      Tasks:
          Knowledge
          Dexterity
          Modular production system
          Continued learning
          Guide to the key principles
          Coaching
      Interpersonal relations:
          Communication that facilitates work, growth, participation, and
              continued learning through the use of psycho-sociological
              games that emphasize understanding and the harmonizing of
              behavioral strategies
      Team operation:
          Objectives to achieve
          Conducting meetings
          Consensus-based decision making
          Conflict resolution
          Intramodular meetings
          Evaluation of the module or team dynamic
      Management:
          Scope of responsibilities
          Information required for decision making
          Development of systemic thinking (relationship between internal
              suppliers and customers)
          Promoting creativity
          Continued improvement, among others through problem solving
 III. Integrate the facilitation of human resource development into the orga-
      nizational structure and strategy
      Development phases:
          Creation
          Troubled waters (trial and error)
          Normalization (process standardization)
          Performance

          Evolution in reaction to change:
          Denial
          Resistance
          Exploration
          Engagement
      Development of new roles in the various management tiers:
          Senior management: vision, orientations, and critical success factors
          Factory management: leadership and support
          Supervision: facilitation and coaching

We spend a long time discussing how to convey these concepts to employees. We already dealt with many of these topics during the first 240-hour training, but this time we opt for a much more hands-on approach. Teaching will be provided to small groups of people who already work together. Sessions will be given for an hour a week per team in a meeting room or in the modules on the production site.

We want it to be done right this time. So we agree that until the second wave of training is done and the concepts are firmly anchored in our employees' minds, the facilitator will remain employed with us.

Pierre-Paul stays with us for nearly two years. He gets deeply involved in eliminating communication problems within the modules and creating a good, healthy working environment. He coaches the seamstresses to accept each other's flaws and focus more on each other's assets. I consider Pierre-Paul's facilitation help to be a key element of the project's success.

FROM SUPERVISOR TO COACH: A CHANGING POSITION

Among traditional management functions, the most undervalued and thankless one is that of supervisor or foreman. But in the change process we've undertaken, this position needs to transform in a profound way.

The Foreman: Caught between a Rock and a Hard Place

In the past, factories used to promote their best employees to the position of first-line supervisor. It was enough for workers to put their hearts into the work, have a good attitude and a good attendance record, and from one day to the next they'd end up in charge. Often, their work experience helped them make decisions, but a lack of training for this new role and a lack of leadership sometimes placed them in very uncomfortable situations. As a result, foremen often had major human resources difficulties.

But in a Lean context, supervisors no longer have a traditional function or the old responsibilities. The teams they supervise are multidisciplinary and much more autonomous. For this reason, in the new environment, we talk about coaches more than foremen.

And if there is a key point in Lean implementation, I'd say that it's the strength, conviction, and dynamic attitude of the first-line supervisors who act as coaches. As a result, we need to carefully analyze the motivation of potential coaches because their leadership and communication skills will help enormously in making a successful transition happen. If the supervisor isn't convinced or convincing, how will the employees react?

Unfortunately, it's not enough to simply give a "coach" title to a former supervisor to make them into one. In practice, what can we do with good foremen who provided valuable service to the company for many years before we moved into Lean? Do we have to recycle them, train them, or demote them? Before making a decision in one direction or another, the first question to ask is: can your current supervisors help you achieve your Lean objectives? If the answer is no, you'll have a difficult decision to make, but it will be a key one in your project's success. You alone can judge for your own situation.

Moving from Supervisor to Coach: A Difficult Transition

I'd like to clarify that I've always had great respect for the supervisors with whom I've worked. They are the first managers in the company to have to make good decisions quickly, because taking a risk to proceed with production on a defective machine or accepting pieces of questionable quality, for instance, can lead to heavy consequences and have a major impact on all other levels of management.

As well, we know that traditional supervisors are perceived as bosses who dictate to employees what they have to do and how to do it, but their roles are very different in a Lean system where the teams are self-managed and where workers must take the time to talk among themselves and come to a consensus about how to proceed. It can make for a difficult situation for old-school supervisors. Overnight, they see their authority reduced, and their decisions challenged and rethought by their work teams. They may feel undermined or irrelevant. If they haven't been properly prepared to deal with these situations, they may find the change too radical and lose all interest in seeing it succeed; they'll worry about their future and their career with the company.

In our case, we have four excellent supervisors. One is a man approaching his 60s who supervises cutting (leather, nylon, and felt) and a team of 20 employees, 95% of whom are men. He opts for early retirement instead of taking complementary courses. The three other supervisors, all women, share the supervision of leather, nylon, and finishing in the sewing section. They're aged 45 to 50. Model employees, devoted and respected by their subordinates, they have acquired solid practical sewing experience since the start of their careers. I have a deep appreciation for the results they've achieved in their departments. They have created a climate of mutual respect and, under their supervision, a level of harmony has reigned in the factory.

In our old work method, these women could accomplish their tasks and assume their responsibilities blindfolded. They had enough experience to be able to handle with confidence the various problems that arose. But the new order of things has thrown them off. Their roles and responsibilities have radically changed. Just like their employees who are learning to work standing up and in teams, using a number of new machines they've never tried before, the supervisors are also undergoing a major shift in their work habits. And, as we have discussed, they've already taken 80 hours of classes specific to their function in addition to the 240 hours of training given to the seamstresses, which should have prepared them to take on their new tasks. But as I see the working climate deteriorate in modules and the productivity level drop, I have my doubts as to their ability to make a culture change of the scope we've undertaken and still maintain the pace. As far as I'm concerned, they need to prove their determination and their faith in this new management philosophy.

Monique, the plant manager, in contrast, has a lot of faith in her supervisors. She hopes that with the training they've received and their solid background, they'll succeed in surmounting the obstacles. Because Monique always likes to give people a second chance, and because I want to respect her attempts, we choose to keep them in position and continue to coach them.

Unfortunately, my doubts turn out to be valid. Despite her hopes, Monique also sees the evidence: the old supervisors aren't measuring up, even if they are making plenty of sacrifices, as well as doing overtime hours at the factory and at home to plan the modules' work (at the end of the first training, when production was about to kick off again, our module management IT (information technology) systems weren't ready yet). None of them stay on. In the first two years of the new system's implementation, they understand that the job is no longer the same in any way. The environment has changed too much, and the pressure to produce on time is too high. The first supervisor takes burnout leave, and the second follows close on her heels. The third, overwhelmed by the events, asks her own boss to replace her. Because these three supervisors are model employees, we find them other jobs, within the company, that suit them better.

Choosing Supervisors Who Have What It Takes to Coach

So we're back at square one. We need to find a brand-new team of coaches from among our staff, and train them.

However, our situation is far from unique. In many cases, especially for supervisors who have held their positions for more than 10 years, transition is almost impossible. I'm convinced that managers who know their supervisors well can identify the ones who'll survive the change after being properly trained. Depending on their leadership style, they can forecast the supervisors' behavior in a teamwork environment.

The secret to choosing a good coach is to make sure the candidate has a few essential qualities. To evaluate a person's coaching potential, a few questions should be asked, such as

1. Is he/she a good communicator? Does he/she fully understand the management's mission and objectives in order to convey them to the teams? Does he/she know how to listen and understand employees' needs and messages? Does he/she have the qualities to facilitate the exchange of ideas, and to facilitate and lead meetings? Does he/she provide good feedback to the proposals made by employees? Is he/she a good negotiator?
2. Is he/she a good leader? Does he/she have the ability to guide a team? Can he/she impress this new culture on them with honesty and respect for others? Can he/she have a positive influence on the employees, especially in conflict situations? Is he/she able to strengthen the employees' sense of pride, responsibility, and self-esteem?
3. Is he/she a good manager? Does he/she have the qualities needed to supervise and evaluate teams, plan and organize meetings, and get a handle on difficult employees? Does he/she understand the importance of psychology in the workplace and in human relations? Can he/she train the employees? Like any good manager, can he/she effectively measure the work teams' performance and help them reach their objectives?

As well, one needs some humility to be a good coach. Have you ever seen or heard a professional sports coach take credit for a victory? It's the athletes the coach leads who produce the victories. But it's common to see a team with a number of star players lose because of a coach's bad strategy, or because of a lack of preparation, conviction, motivation, or communication.

You can probably tell that a good coach is a rare delicacy! If you have one or more in your organization, take good care of them! Above all, don't forget that they're the ones providing a link between senior management and the production employees, and that they have a very difficult role to play.

After establishing the attitudes required of a good coach, we insist, during the training courses for supervisors that follow, that they need to learn how to handle the employees they're in charge of. The coaches must help the employees reach their full potential by focusing their work on technical development (sewing) and social development (interactions between the members of the various teams). The coach must be able to identify each team member's strengths and weaknesses, and work with them along their path. As they say, two heads are better than one! By focusing everyone's efforts on a common goal, we can only improve our performance.

Chapter 9

Establishing a Gain-Sharing System to Stimulate Productivity

APRIL 1994

The group bonus program presented to the factory committee in 1993 replaced the piecework system. But a year later, we are forced to note that it's not suitable for the production philosophy we want for our factory.

A BONUS SYSTEM THAT GETS IN THE WAY OF THE OBJECTIVE

The group bonus system we set up last year is based on product quality, team efficiency, and team members' work attendance. They measure their performance against production standards established using the Methods-Time Measurement* (MTM) method. Any performance exceeding the 100% standard generates salary savings that are shared between the modules: 1% performance above the standard represents an extra 1% salary to share among the team members.

The system also includes a self-regulation mechanism. First, quality errors must be corrected, without additional remuneration, by the same module that's responsible for them. So it's in the teams' interest to do the work well on the first try. Then, when a module's employee is absent, they're not replaced, which reduces the team's performance and gain; as a result, this encourages employees to have strong attendance. The standards are only revised when an absence is justifiable.

The teams' efficiency is surprising. At this pace, the learning curve is proving to be shorter than expected.

I should be very pleased with these results but when I tour the modules, I sense that something's not quite right. It turns out I'm onto something: since our new start with module-based production, the orders are piling up so fast that we've been gripped with a sort of panic. This year, we're experiencing one of the biggest-ever expansions in sales, especially to the United States. This explosion makes it difficult for us to satisfy the demand. Stressed out by the ever-growing number of orders and the problems with the learning pace, our seamstresses discreetly abandon rotation and come back to their specializations and the machines they master the best. The supervisors turn a blind eye to this state of affairs because the teams' efficiency jumps overnight. The seamstresses have less pressure to deal with, and they start to accumulate bonuses! The employees have found a loophole in the system: our new program has become nothing more than a common team piecework bonus! As a result of all this, we've more or less managed to deliver the orders on time but the number of work accidents has increased considerably. The lure of profit has taken precedence over our new management philosophy.

So we decide to put an end to the bonus system just a year after introducing it, as it goes against our ultimate goal.

NEED FOR A GAIN-SHARING MODEL

When we decide to implement a new bonus system, we first take a look at existing models. No need to reinvent the wheel: there are already a number of well-documented, productivity-based sharing methods.

Sharing Plan Based on Productivity

When our examination of various profit-sharing systems is well under way, we then need to determine the basis for calculation that suits us best: profits or productivity increases. Upon reflection, the latter option seems the only logical one, for the following reasons:

1. Genfoot doesn't do individual accounting (grand ledger) for each of its factories, as they are not considered profit centers. The company's profitability is consolidated. However, our accounting systems are detailed enough for controls related to the factories' productivity.
2. Because the company is private, its financial reports are confidential. However, the factories' internal accounting is open to the managers and members of the factory committees.
3. If a factory is productive, its employees can receive bonuses even if the company as a whole is not profitable. This is a double-edged sword for Genfoot but in our case, it's the only viable option.

4. While it's difficult to read a summary and interpret that data, it's even more difficult to do so for employees who aren't used to doing so. As well, the long waiting period between the end of a fiscal year and the auditing of the financial statements could be a demotivating factor for the workers.
5. An increase in sale price could boost the company's profits without it being more productive.

For all these reasons, especially the final one, we prefer the productivity gain-sharing system.

I have some experience in this area because I had the opportunity to evaluate these sharing plans for several months at one of my previous jobs.

*****

In 1982, when I was working with Electrolux®, I was determined to convince my bosses to get rid of piecework. I succeeded in getting approval to attend an international conference organized by masters of the subject in Washington, in the United States.

During my trip, day after day I devoured original and interesting information. I heard one success story after another from world-renowned companies, such as Rockwell International, Bell & Howell, Firestone, TRW, and many others. Right away I saw the impact of this kind of culture change and the benefits my employer and all the company's employees could reap from it. I also realized that our performance bonus system was unfair because only the direct labor force was eligible for it. The others weren't, even though they made up more than 20% of employees paid by the hour. Manual and electric lift truck drivers, recycling service employees, packagers, shippers, mold setters and others, they all clearly contributed to productivity improvement in their factories and to the company's success, and all this without bonuses! It was clear that we couldn't continue to function effectively in an individualist work environment.

During the conference, then, I focused on the three productivity-sharing plans that were best known at the time: the Scanlon, Rucker, and Improshare plans[*]. I remember, in particular, being very impressed with one of the lectures and the discussion that followed it, given by Mitchell Fein, the creator of Improshare, who was very convincing with his approach.

*****

The Scanlon, Rucker, and Improshare plans are all of interest and have some basic points in common:

• They are all based on productivity.
• They focus on groups and not on individuals.

---

[*] The three plans are explained in detail in the Appendix.

- They measure productivity with "macro" elements rather than only the "micro" ones that are considered in detailed and costly exercises such as time and movement studies. When done well, however, the micro ones can serve as a base for the calculation of cost price.
- They encourage teamwork, cooperation, and the participation of all the company's employees toward a common objective.
- They always split the profits resulting from productivity improvement between the employee and the employer.

To apply a plan of this scope to productivity at Genfoot, we must be sure that we're measuring the right activities. This is where it becomes crucial to precisely define the term "productivity." To do this, we decide to use a fairly simple formula:

$$\text{Productivity} = \frac{\text{Output}}{\text{Input}} \qquad (9.1)$$

In manufacturing, output is expressed by the number of pieces produced by a group or team covered by the sharing plan, while input represents the number of employees "used" (or the resources consumed) to produce the output.

By limiting ourselves to a brief and simple definition of productivity, we can transmit the information to our employees in a more understandable way.

After analyzing the options available to us, we come to the step of selecting the plan with which everyone will be most comfortable. At this stage of the project, it is clear that the employees need to take part in choosing and implementing the plan. We expect that a combination of the various existing programs will be the solution of choice. One thing is for sure: the plan we choose must be easy for everyone to understand and use. Nothing too complicated, just a program that's fair and effective!

An Employer/Employee Committee to Put the Plan into Action

We create a special committee to analyze the pros and cons of the various programs and to help us implement one. The mixed 17-person committee, made up of management and employees, must develop a gain-sharing policy, and an ad hoc development and writing subcommittee is in charge of evaluating suggestions. The committee includes one representative from each department.

The committee's first job is to find a name for itself. Similar to a sports team, the name will help identify the group and rally its members. We study a few suggestions before arriving at a consensus. We finally pick the acronym IMPACT, in which each letter symbolizes a key concept for the program: **I**nitiative, **M**otivation, **P**articipation, **A**melioration, (Improvement), **C**ommunication, **T**eamwork.

Next, we clarify our mission and objectives. They are as follows:

- Mission: "Establish a gain-sharing system that recognizes the efforts that everyone makes toward productivity, quality, and continued improvement."
- Objectives:
  - Share the financial gains that flow from productivity improvement at the factory.
  - Promote a climate of total engagement and employee participation in the factory's success.
  - Remain more productive and more competitive while offering a superior-quality product.
  - Improve communication between management and employees.
  - Improve employee morale while encouraging teamwork.
  - Reduce expenses.

Two employees are elected by each department to sit on the IMPACT committee for a one-year term. Exceptionally, at the end of the first year, one of the two employees will stay in their position for a second term in order to provide continuity. The committee meets at least once a month, in the first week, to summarize the month that just passed. The employee representatives adopt the slogan "Take to heart what you used to take by the hour."

We next establish a list of benefits that both employees and employer can enjoy when the gain-sharing program is in place. For the employees, the benefits are as follows:

- Greater employment security resulting from higher factory productivity
- Improved communication
- Increased recognition and merit
- Benefits directly linked to productivity
- Sense of contributing to the company's success
- Deeper knowledge of the company, its successes, and its problems
- Improvement in relations between employees (factory-supervision-management)
- Stronger self-appreciation

For the employer, the benefits are just as appealing:

- Improvement in productivity via cost reduction and boosted production
- Employees' identification with the company, its goals, and its problems
- Improvement in problem detection and resolution
- Access to ideas and renewed efforts
- Improvement in work relations
- Promotion of an efficient work environment, as well as communication and teamwork skills
- Increase in the organization's flexibility

At the next stage, we list the possible sources of productivity gains and explain the way to calculate and share them. To work, the system must be very simple, easy to verify, and well understood by all employees. We have two different indicators that translate the factory's performance into financial terms. Those are the productivity ratio and the ratio of controllable costs.

Productivity increases depend directly on the quantity of merchandise produced, salaries paid, and other factory expenses.

Each month, we calculate the productivity ratio using the following formula:

$$\text{Productivity ratio} = \frac{\text{Salaries paid}}{\text{Quantity produced} \times \text{standard unit time}} \quad (9.2)$$

There's a gain when the month's ratio is less than the annual objective expressed in dollars per minute of work ($/min). The productivity ratio is indexed annually to take into account inflation and salary increases.

The ratio of controllable costs is determined based on expenses. Every year, we set an operating budget for the factory. It includes all the costs incurred in product manufacturing, be they fixed (rent, taxes, insurance, etc.) or variable (electricity, heating, maintenance, etc.). Some are proportional to consumption and act directly on gains. The only costs included in the ratio of controllable costs are the ones that employees can influence. Here's the list:

- Indirect labor and supervision
- Office employee salaries
- Product development (materials)
- Building maintenance
- Machinery maintenance
- Heating and electricity
- Telephone and courier services
- Travel
- Office supplies

Gains are shared in equal parts between the factory employees and the company. Half of the employees' share is given directly to them, and the other half is put aside to cover possible future losses. At the end of the year, if the reserve balance is positive, it's distributed in its entirety to employees; if not, the company absorbs the losses and resets the counter to zero.

Apart from the reserve, the gains associated with controllable costs, compiled and posted monthly, are distributed twice a year, in June (before annual vacations) and in December (before Christmas). These dates offer the double advantage of meeting the employees' wishes while coinciding with our fiscal year quarters (monthly payments would have engendered useless expense and loss of time). The bonuses are based on the total of the past six months. As such, 50% of a given month's gain can be canceled out by a subsequent loss. The six-month interval eliminates any artificial bonus reduction resulting from seasonal expenses, such as air conditioning, heating, and so forth.

Regardless of the frequency at which bonuses are paid out, in a productivity gain-sharing program, it's crucial to calculate productivity ratios each month, even each week, because that's what the whole factory's staff is trying to beat. This continued feedback is essential for motivating employees. Publishing the ratios has a positive influence on all operations, regardless of the results: a disappointing month encourages employees to renew their efforts, and a positive month inspires further achievement.

Unlike regular pay, which is paid by direct deposit, the bonuses are always paid by check. We believe that when employees receive physical proof of their accomplishments, it reinforces the reward. For practical reasons, payment of any amount less than $50 is carried over to the next share.

The productivity ratios and controllable costs are revised every year. The new objectives are based on the average of the last five years[*] and indexed to inflation:

$$\text{Ratio } 2002 = \frac{\text{Ratio } 2001 + \text{Ratio } 2000 + \cdots + \text{Ratio } 1997}{5} \qquad (9.3)$$

To determine who gets a bonus, we develop the following policy:

1. To be eligible, a regular or seasonal employee must accomplish an exclusion period of 1,500 hours of full-time or part-time work.
2. Employees who resign after completing the exclusion period and who are rehired must first work 300 hours before becoming eligible once again.
3. Employees who resign without completing the 1,500 regulation hours and who are rehired must start the exclusion period over.
4. Employees reassigned from one department to another are not penalized.
5. Employees who move from one factory to another are considered beginners.

The individual bonuses are prorated to each person's hours worked, which discourages absenteeism and encourages people to respect safety standards (employees on sick leave don't earn bonuses).

After Two Years, a Mitigated Report on Shared Gains

The results of the first two years of the sharing plan's application are fairly timid, as shown in Table 9.1. Faced with these numbers, the employees are fairly discouraged. They find that the gains are minimal, and they're

TABLE 9.1 Gains Shared in 1995 and 1996

Year	Total Gain	Employee Share	
1995	$11,024	$5,512	$0.02/h
1996	$17,380	$8,690	$0.04/h

[*] In the first years, we work with the earlier data that's available.

still comparing them with their earlier performance bonuses, which were much higher.

Monique and I see things differently. Personally, I'm disappointed that our modular system isn't producing the way it should. The teams have made too many small changes, which prevent the modules from producing more. I'm well aware that with corrections, the gain-sharing plan would be more profitable for both parties. The factory manager agrees with my observations because she also can see a lot of *muda** at every step of production. It's clear to us that we need to undertake a major change or the situation could undermine the system's credibility.

ADJUSTING OUR AIM

The major change we envision must happen at the very bottom of the pyramid, with employee training. We realize that the basics of our new philosophy haven't been acquired solidly enough, and that they've never been reinforced since the transformations we introduced four years prior. So we decide to set off down the path once again. Monique restructures the production department and sets a schedule for new theory and hands-on courses.

As well, the change process aims to fix problems that are related to the constant rise in workplace accidents, lax supervision, and the lack of team harmony.

New Just-in-Time Training to Get Employees Involved

Monique and Rita decide to teach the new classes themselves. They meet with all the teams and the supervisors to re-explain just-in-time* (JIT) principles to them (see Photo 9.1).

We write a four-page document that summarizes, in very simple terms, the elements we feel are key to ensuring the success of JIT implementation. The document serves as a base for the theory training.

We list the main changes that go along with this new philosophy as we concretely apply them when we manufacture products. Table 9.2 provides a few examples.

We remind the employees of the advantages of JIT by making sure we convince them of all its benefits. We insist on each of the points set out here and make sure they're well understood by the team members. Each person must

- Avoid repetitive movements
- Move around so as not to stay in the same position for too long
- Acquire a level of versatility
- Minimize the stock of work in process
- Acquire more flexibility
- Reduce the manufacturing and response time
- Establish better relationships within the work teams

PHOTO 9.1 Rita explaining JIT principles as applied to our production.

TABLE 9.2 Examples of Changes Made through JIT Implementation

Old Philosophy	New Philosophy
Assembly done in lines, individually.	Assembly done in modules, collectively.
The bigger the lots, the higher the productivity.	The smaller the lots, the higher the flexibility.
We stock so as not to run out.	We stock the minimum and do preventative maintenance.
I operate my machine, and I do it alone.	I work with a team; together we produce quality.
My method is the best.	I'm trained in JIT, like everyone; they help me understand the process and encourage me to use it.
I'm very fast and I get bonuses, regardless of my colleagues' efficiency.	My team's production capacity is determined by the slowest seamstress, so we have to help her improve.

As well, this time, we teach them the prerequisites for the system's success, which each person needs to take on:

- Learning new operations
- Partially maintaining the machines
- Controlling quality autonomously
- Working with a team spirit
- Carrying out certain planning tasks

- Contributing to the continued improvement of all activities
- Stopping work, if necessary, to fix problems with safety, product quality, or machine reliability

Before explaining how to get there, we briefly go over the steps of JIT implementation:

1. We (the employer) have finished reorganizing the factory and training the modules. The work is done standing up, and we have already provided the additional machines necessary for the system to work properly.
2. Rotation and learning the other operations already make for versatility. This step is key to working in modules.
3. We need to encourage teamwork. The presence of a facilitator has helped expose and talk about internal problems within the teams.
4. The final step consists of reducing the stock of work in process. We must get to the point of circulating one pair at a time, from one machine to the next, from hand-to-hand.

Finally, we insist on the fact that to succeed with the implementation, we absolutely must respect the following rules; they are *sine qua non* conditions.

1. Have only one pair in hand at a time.
2. Respect the sequence of operations and change the machines' position at each change of model.
3. Carry out operations in order until the next occupied machine, and leave the pair to the seamstress working on that machine.
4. Go get a new pair from the hands of the person preceding you as soon as you hand a pair to a colleague or finish the one you're working on.
5. Eliminate crossover movements.
6. Leave pieces in place during work breaks (break, lunch, and so forth).
7. Take on several tasks within the module.
8. Leave your place as soon as the next person asks you to, without even finishing the operation you're working on.
9. Signal any problems that cause delays within the team.
10. As needed, stop all the module's activities and fix the problem.

Practical training comes after we present these four pages of theory.

Through hand-to-hand simulation that takes no more than two hours, we address all the problems that can be encountered in production. The practice takes place in the *gemba*, meaning the modules; we prefer to do the exercise with real components and real machines because it's very different from experimenting in a classroom. This way, the problems that come up are corrected immediately. During the training, Monique and I remind them that in 1992, a trainer used little paper boats for the same simulation, and we joke that the boats sank like the *Titanic* on their first expedition... . But this time, the teams that already took the training and are already working with the hand-to-hand model are making immense progress. The seamstresses even begin to enjoy using the method. Watching them work, it looks as if they were discovering it for the first time. What did they do with the 240 hours of training they received four years earlier? This is proof that ongoing training is crucial!

Spectacular but Fragile Results

In the following year, when I assess all the changes we've made and their results, I see that our productivity is progressing considerably from one month to the next. For me, the theory and practical training, the active participation of the IMPACT and PREMUS* committees, and the work of the facilitator are all finally beginning to bear fruit.

After one year, we observe a change that borders on the miraculous. We are finally reaping what we sowed: the gains to be shared move from $17,000 in 1996 to $877,868 in 1997! The employees' share is at $438,934, or $1.11 per hour. Distributed in mid-December, these amounts ensure a very merry Christmas! Even the most skeptical employees are now convinced of the value of JIT.

How can we explain this spectacular jump if not for the generalized implementation of rotation and hand-to-hand? The result makes me think that when the project began, we should perhaps have imposed them, rather than letting the teams decide on what method to follow.

Our flexibility is such that we can now produce three or four orders for different customers in the same module, on the same day. In other words, we've reached our initial goal! Or almost. Our new system is so well-liked that our customers start to order in smaller quantities, more frequently, which complicates our job. I realize at this point that we're victims of our own success.

Indeed, success has its dangers. After this first year of massive gains, the employees, thinking that the exploit will be easy to repeat, let themselves relax a bit. The more frequent model changes and the recruitment of new employees also contribute to bringing down our productivity and oblige us to keep on top of backslides in the learning curve year after year. And in fact, the gains are less substantial. All of a sudden, discontent rears its head once again.

In any case, this confirms that it's much more difficult to stay ahead of the game than it is to get there in the first place. I had thought that the principle of continuous improvement would have helped us avoid this kind of problem. If not, why should we make additional efforts when we're just running to stand still?

REVISION OF THE PRODUCTIVITY GAIN-SHARING PLAN

Faced with the disappointing results of the previous fiscal year, and to address the discontent among the most motivated employees, the IMPACT committee

---

* The PREMUS committee was created to work on the question of musculoskeletal problems.

asks us to review the gain-sharing system in order to make it more equitable for the modules that are working at full tilt and producing at 100%.

At the beginning of implementation, we had planned to revise the gain-sharing plan after five years, and we are now at the threshold of year 5, so we decide it's a good time to tackle the problem.

Seeking a New, More Equitable Gain-Sharing System

Similar to our old piecework remuneration system, there are always employees who are more gifted, more dexterous, more conscientious, or more motivated than others, who excel just as well alone as with a team—but they don't take kindly to the idea of sharing their bonuses with those who are lagging behind. We often hear comments such as, "Our team works very hard to beat the ratio, while others drag their feet. We're working for them!" Even the supervisors complain that their colleagues aren't pushing their employees enough to excel. As well, some departments have always worked better than others, just by the nature of their operations. They find themselves at a disadvantage in the unique team context we've put into place.

The IMPACT committee's request leads us to reconsider the base principle we used to establish the sharing plan: we wanted to get buy-in from *all* the factory's employees, whether they were direct, indirect, or management. So we decided that the team bonus would be shared equally between all the employees, prorated by their accumulated work-hours. In other words, in our view, the entire factory would form a single team united in a common goal: productivity improvement.

This is why I have, until now, been opposed to the idea of sharing gains by activity, as some employees request, because I always dream of a united factory in which employees and supervisors help each other to reach the best possible productivity. For me, approving inequalities in the gain-sharing now means coming back to the individualism that's typical of piecework.

That said, I'm aware that it's unfair for the teams that excel when they see their efforts mitigated or brought down by less-motivated people. As a result, after the gains drop radically by 60% in 1998, I resign myself to making a change to the gain-sharing method. But how can we be fair to everyone without discouraging the best? How do we protect those who work on more complex or difficult tasks without rewarding idleness?

After considering these questions for a number of weeks, we present a new sharing plan at the monthly IMPACT committee meeting. The new plan, more complicated but in our opinion more logical, takes into account the productivity of each department and team. The calculation's complexity comes from the fact that the workforce is shared among the various departments and areas. The plan proposes a gain distribution that will more accurately reflect the impact of a given employee on the group's performance.

As illustrated in Figure 9.1, our plan groups employees into four categories:

1. Employees linked to a team: all the members of a module.
2. Employees linked to a department: cutters, handlers, supervisors, mechanics.
3. Employees linked to a work shift: shippers, inspectors.
4. Employees linked to the factory: warehouse operators, office staff, engineers.

The sharing varies based on the categories to which the employees belong. In the first category, the team's efficiency represents 15% of the overall evaluation; that of the department to which the team is attached, 30%; and that of the factory as a whole, 55%. As such, the team is rewarded for its efforts (the employees are happy), so is the department (the supervisor is satisfied), and we preserve team spirit within the large team that is the factory. In the second category, the factory's overall result determines 55% of total gain, and the service, 45%. In the third category, 55% of the gain comes from the factory's results and 45% from the work shift. In the fourth category, the gain is a function of the entire factory's results, like it was calculated before the gain-sharing model was revamped.

Before even presenting the reform, I start feeling proud of it. All the factory's employees will find their realities reflected here. This new way of working is much fairer toward the good workers without eliminating the principle of the full team. So, I am really not expecting what comes next.

A Surprise from the Employees

To conclude the process, we present the new differential gain-sharing calculation at an IMPACT committee meeting. To our great surprise, after consulting the factory's employees, the committee advises us that the employees have unanimously rejected it in favor of keeping the system that's already in place. It seems that the concept of "one equal factory, one team" has sunk in!

But the committee members also suggest solutions to a few problems that are hindering their productivity: among others, a school module to facilitate the integration of new employees and, in slow periods, the opportunity for seamstresses to change departments to familiarize themselves with other types of sewing machines. Finally, there's a final suggestion I like a lot. In speaking with a supervisor about inefficient modules, an employee says, "When you see a team dragging its heels, what are you waiting for to give them a kick in the pants?"

By the end of the meeting, I come out with a very clear message. I see, in this last bit—which might seem like just an anecdote, but which is masking much more—a sort of cry for help. Is it possible that the supervisors aren't doing their job properly, or is this just a discipline problem? Are the supervisors letting employees get away with laziness? Do they need to be stricter, even give some people a talking-to? Have they really understood their new role as coaches? (The facilitator we bring in helps out with these questions; see Chapter 8.)

	Portion of Hours Worked during the Month					Distribution of Hours Worked
	Factory	Shift	Department	Module	TOTAL	
Module	55%		30%	15%	100%	Module 15% 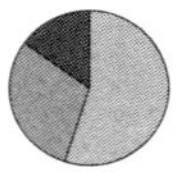 Department 30% Factory 55%
All members of a module Example: One month (4 weeks at 39 h = 156 h) Calculation	85.8 h (0.55 × 156)		46.8 h (0.30 × 156)	23.4 h (0.15 × 156)	156 h	
Linked to a department	55%		45%		100%	Department 45% 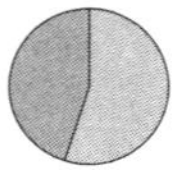 Factory 55%
Supervisors, mechanics, handlers, prefits, cutters Example: One month (4 weeks at 39 h = 156 h) Calculation	85.8 h (0.55 × 156)		70.2 h (0.45 × 156)		156 h	
Linked to a work shift	55%	45%			100%	Shift 45%  Factory 55%
Shipping, receiving, inspectors (quality) Example: One month (4 weeks at 39 h = 156 h) Calculation	85.8 h (0.55 × 156)	70.2 h (0.45 × 156)			156 h	
Factory	100%				100%	Factory 100% 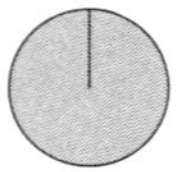
Warehouse operator, head mechanic, samples, stock management, quality control, production clerks, engineers Example: One month (4 weeks at 39 h = 156 h) Calculation	156 h				156 h	

FIGURE 9.1 Portions of hours attributed based on employee type.

I notice that I'm enjoying these meetings more and more, first because I've always wanted to be close to the employees, and second because I really like the dynamic that's emerged. The committee members trust us now, and it's reciprocal.

REPORT THAT INSPIRES VIGILANCE

Our productivity gain*-sharing plan is based on a standard dollars/work-minute ratio. At the start of each fiscal year, we determine a new ratio to beat. The first two years of the program are very difficult because the seamstresses aren't practicing hand-to-hand in the modules. But starting with the day the factory manager decided to impose the method on all the seamstresses, the dam broke. Productivity increased to a point that amounts ranging from $500,000 to $1,000,000 are being distributed to the employees. Starting then, people's trust in the Lean*/JIT system, which was pretty weak, firmed up for good. This success, far from instant, is the end result of many years on a path strewn with obstacles. Happily, senior management's support never wavered.

As shown in the numbers in Table 9.3, our results improve from one year to the next from 1998 to 2000. That said, it's clear that with the improvements, it's becoming more and more difficult to beat our records. As they say, you can't squeeze blood from a stone. This highlights the fact that any productivity gain-sharing model must be reconsidered periodically. Sometimes you just need to make a small change, an addition or subtraction of one or more activities, to reinvigorate it and help it fly again. In our case, we had estimated a 5- to 10-year interval for reevaluating our program.

The plan runs out of steam and the gains are thinning in the seventh year of implementation. Because we certainly don't want to lose the cruising speed we've taken three years to reach, some small readjustments are made to give the program a second wind.

TABLE 9.3 Productivity Sharing Numbers for Years 1998 to 2000

Year	Gain	Employee Share	
1998	$364,228	$182,144	$0.35/h
1999	$350,200	$175,100	$0.83/h
2000	$528,800	$264,400	$0.60/h*

* Although gain was highest in 2000, the number of employees had increased, hence the employee share per hour was lower.

Chapter 10

Carrying Out a First Assessment and Detecting Errors along the Way

JANUARY 1999

At this stage of implementation, we have already succeeded beyond our wildest hopes, despite a few mistakes along the way. In a project of this scope, mistakes happen often, especially when the experiment is undertaken using internal resources, without much reliance on external expertise or consultants. In particular, we notice—and this isn't unusual—that we have somewhat underestimated the following points:

1. The length of the learning curve
2. The effect of bottlenecks
3. The scope of the information technology (IT) adjustments required
4. The length of time to implement hand-to-hand

LENGTH OF THE LEARNING CURVE

Recall that our initial objective was to complete the factory's transformation in three months and then implement hand-to-hand in all the modules within three years. In the meantime, we would have continued to coach our teams to bring them to 100% performance. At base, three years seemed sufficient for the learning curve on the new machines.

But as things proceed, we realize that we've underestimated the learning-related difficulties. The most revealing example of our mistake is the following.

We were convinced that an operator with better than 100% performance on one type of sewing machine could master a new type of machine in three years at most. In our view, sewing couldn't be that different from one machine to the next. But the reality is very different indeed. Each machine has its particularities: the number of needles and their placement, the type of stitch, the accessories such as automatic thread-cutters, and so forth. Each of these small details complicates the employees' acquisition of automatic habits and extends the length of time it takes to learn how the machines work. The most experienced seamstresses seem even more disoriented than the apprentices!

Another factor that contributed to extending the time was the full integration of packers into the modules, which we couldn't have predicted at the start.

At the start of the implementation project, packaging was a function distinct from sewing in the module; the packers were at the end of the cycle and didn't rotate. They simply tagged the boots, cleaned them as needed, and packaged them. But their hourly wage was $2 less than that of the seamstresses. This motivated a packer to ask us permission to learn how to sew outside her normal work hours. After 40 hours of practice, we integrated her into the module's rotation. She continued to progress while she worked. After 1,000 hours of work, she moved up to the seamstress wage. This initiative encouraged the other 35 packers to follow in her footsteps. Two years later, the packaging job no longer existed in the factory; the task is now the sewing team's responsibility.

But, all in all, even though the change led to a temporary drop in efficiency within the modules and a longer learning curve, we are very pleased with the turn of events.

We met our objectives after five years of production. Once this period was over, any seamstress from any department could work any machine in any module and hit her full performance before the end of a workday.

Patience is rewarded!

EFFECT OF BOTTLENECKS

For modular production to work well, the machine-to-employee ratio should be nearly two-to-one. However, when we kicked off production again after the first training, we had to deal with two unavoidable realities:

1. To respect the ideal machine-to-employee ratio, we'd have had to buy several additional sewing machines, especially because we had to fill an increased number of orders. We knew this. But because Genfoot is an SME (small and medium enterprise) and had already invested major money in the transition to JIT* (just in time) and *Kaizen*, we couldn't afford that kind of expense at the time.
2. We had to respect our promise not to lay off any workers whose jobs had been abolished as part of the restructuring.

So we had to produce with eight seamstresses per module, even though each of the modules was only equipped with 10 machines. The workers didn't have enough room to maneuver, and rotation was difficult to do. There was a lot of waiting *muda** for the sewing machines, and the problem was accentuated by the fact that, in the first months, the seamstresses weren't as efficient with the machines they didn't know as well. Operations were synchronized to within a few seconds, but that wasn't enough to prevent bottlenecks.

*****

Let's take a fictional example to illustrate our imbalance problem and its damaging effects on productivity.

In a module, three distinct sewing operations are carried out by three different workers according to the following cycles:

Operation 1: 30 seconds
Operation 2: 50 seconds
Operation 3: 40 seconds

The first seamstress produces more quickly than the second, and the third has to wait for the second to finish before proceeding, so there's necessarily stocking *muda* between the two first operations and waiting *muda* between the second and third operations.

Now let's take a look, in numbers, at the bottlenecks' impact on productivity. For this group of employees carrying out three successive operations, the longest operation (Operation 2) determines the length of the cycle for the production of one item. Operation 2 requires 50 seconds, so the group's output is 72 pairs per hour (or per 3,600 seconds):

$$3,600 \text{ s/h} \div 50 \text{ s/pair} = 72 \text{ pairs/h} \tag{10.1}$$

By dividing the result by the number of employees involved in the production of each piece, which is to say 3, we get an average output per seamstress of 24 items per hour.

To compare, let's now calculate the output of a versatile employee who performs all three operations, one after the other. The total cycle length per piece is 120 seconds (30 seconds for the first operation, 50 seconds for the second, and 40 seconds for the third), so the seamstress's output would be 30 pairs per hour:

$$3,600 \text{ s/h} \div 120 \text{ s/pair} = 30 \text{ pairs/h} \tag{10.2}$$

Her average output per hour would then be 25% higher than that of each seamstress in the first example.

*****

Our seamstresses' individual efficiency was therefore lower in the modules in which eight employees shared the operations than it would have been in modules with fewer, but versatile employees. This is one of the reasons for which the productivity gain-sharing bonuses in the first two years were so low.

The solution was evident: because we couldn't increase the number of machines, we had to eliminate the imbalance produced by the bottleneck by reducing the number of seamstresses per module, while respecting our promise not to lay off anyone.

Fortunately, circumstances worked in our favor. During the first year of the new system's implementation, 32 employees decided to take early retirement, so we were able to reduce the number of seamstresses to seven per module. In the two following years, 28 more employees made the same choice. This helped us bring the number of seamstresses down to six, and then five per module. While we hadn't been too strict up to that point, we then began to insist that they systematically practice rotation and hand-to-hand. In doing this, we eliminated the bottlenecks. The seamstresses no longer waited for machines to become available. They just had to tap the shoulder of the one ahead of them so that she could give up her spot and move ahead to the next station.

SCOPE OF THE INFORMATION TECHNOLOGY (IT) ADJUSTMENTS REQUIRED

Information systems and Manufacturing Resources Planning* (MRP) systems are present in nearly every manufacturing environment. Among others, they provide essential services for raw material supply planning and for the establishment of a factory master plan. And while these aspects are important in a push production* setting, they are even more so in a JIT and pull production* setting. In a JIT system, the orders and production lots are smaller but there are many more of them as compared to in a traditional environment; synchronizing them is all the more critical. An MRP-type information system greatly simplifies planning and order monitoring.

It's a myth that MRP systems and *kanban** are mutually exclusive. I'd like to set the record straight: that's not entirely correct. While MRP systems and JIT rest on opposing philosophies, they are still complementary. MRP makes it possible to manage the often-complex Bill of Materials and operation sequences; it also generates the factory's medium-term production plan. JIT, for its part, makes it possible to conduct real-time—even visual—control of our stock using *kanban*, which is a good tool for controlling production movements in a pull production environment.

Before switching to JIT, Genfoot already had an MRP system. Instead of procuring a standardized information system, we chose to use our existing platform to administer all the newly converted factory's activities. But we had to adapt it by grafting on a sort of computerized *kanban* that reflected our new teamwork-based organization.

As well, because the calculation of payroll, bonuses, and production standards had to be done in a totally different way after the transition, our other IT systems also needed to follow.

The IT systems' conversion was a project of crucial importance, for which we unfortunately underestimated the scope. Among other things, we had to rewrite the piece organization programs and find a way to plan production for each of the 40 modules while taking into account the number of employees in each one, each person's name, and the time they took to fill each order. The new programs also had to manage raw material stock and supply the factory using JIT.

The task was colossal for our small IT department with its three employees! When we described our needs to him, six months before the factory converted to JIT, the department director estimated that it would take 12 months to make all the required changes. So the systems weren't ready until six months after the factory's transformation. This had a major impact: in the interval, we had to make all our reports manually. And to complicate and extend our programmers' work, during the first 12 months in the new structure, we kept asking them to adapt the systems thanks to our employees' suggestions. That said, even after the new systems were up and running, we never stopped changing our programs to make them more efficient.

Our mistake was that, from day one, we didn't include the IT department in our preliminary discussions and our draft solutions. We thought it was preferable to experiment a bit first and then present the department with a precise, concise plan. Today we recognize that if we hadn't waited, we could have reduced the IT adaptation process time by several months.

LENGTH OF TIME TO IMPLEMENT HAND-TO-HAND

The last of our mistakes was related to the autonomy we gave the work teams in terms of implementing hand-to-hand. At the beginning of the project, we really stuck to the principle of self-managed teams, and it seemed to make sense to let them integrate hand-to-hand work at their own pace. But experience showed us that although we made that decision with the best intentions, it wasn't the right one.

I mentioned earlier that when we started out working in self-managed teams, some employees rejected full autonomy outright. They preferred that management tell them what to do and how to do it. So they adopted hand-to-hand right away. These employees' modules ended up being the most productive ones, while the modules left to their own process lagged in reaching their efficiency objective.

Of course, in hindsight, we have results and concrete facts that allow us to say, today, that if we had to do it again, we wouldn't hesitate for a second to impose the hand-to-hand system on all the production teams, even if it might have caused more grumbling at the start.

Chapter 11

Putting *Kaizen* into Practice in the Factory

JANUARY 2002

*Kaizen** consists of a multitude of small improvements that we make to our procedures, our organization, and any other *gemba** activity. The principle of small-cost improvements must be sustained and encouraged so that it continues. It's somewhat similar to a circus entertainer who starts by spinning a plate on the end of a stick, and then adds a second, a third, a fourth plate, and so on. He has to return to the first one to give it a new spin and do the same for the rest. He knows very well that if he stops the cycle, the plates will lose their energy and they'll all fall. *Kaizen* works according to the same principle. Once we carry out an improvement project, we have to make sure we don't sit around admiring the result; we need to move on to the next one.

Most of these projects result from workers' ideas—because really, who's better placed than an employee working in production to suggest and implement small improvements? Our duty as administrators is to maintain their motivation by implementing suggestion programs, or productivity profit-sharing or company profit-sharing programs.

Since we implemented the new mode of operation in the factories, we have put a number of *Kaizen* projects into place. We can categorize them according to the investment they required:

- Small *Kaizen*: under $100
- Medium *Kaizen*: between $100 and $1,000
- Big *Kaizen*: over $1,000

The following sections give some examples of these.

EXAMPLES OF SMALL *KAIZEN*

In traditional North American factories, we have the bad habit of always look-ing for the genius idea that will save us thousands or hundreds of thousands of dollars. Searching for this kind of idea can take months or even years. And often, it never comes!

Really, it's small changes that create the savings. At Genfoot, we experi-ence it day after day since we transitioned to *Kaizen*/Lean*: hundreds of small *Kaizen* made daily or weekly by our production employees lead to the greatest savings. We make multiple, continual improvements to our procedures. This is the essence of the *Kaizen* philosophy.

*****

I remember one of my factory tours in Japan where I was very impressed by the simplicity of some ideas and the economic rewards to which they led*. As I wandered down a hall toward a meeting room, I saw all sorts of employee suggestions that had been taken up and implemented by the employer. Photos of the employees who'd made each suggestion were posted alongside a short explanatory text. A sample or mock-up illustrated each idea. I stopped in front of an empty plastic container to see why it was there. The interpreter who was taking care of our group backtracked to ask me politely to come join the others. I couldn't help but point out to him that the container was empty. When he read the Japanese text, he explained with a smile that the separator placed at the one-third mark of the container was an employee suggestion. The separator made it possible to sort two different sizes of parts. The risk of confusing the two part sizes used to complicate the task; that risk had disappeared, thanks to the separator. For an investment of less than $1, the employee had saved the employer $300 a year. Someone just had to think of it!

*****

Thanks to our employees' suggestions, we also regularly implement small-scale new work methods. Here are a few examples.

Adding a Velcro® Strip on the Sewing Machines

> **Problem:** When we need to replace a needle on a sewing machine, the seamstress must rummage through a bin of replacement parts to find a case that contains several needles. She then takes one and puts the case back in its place.
> **Solution:** A needle case is placed within easy reach on the machine itself, using a Velcro strip (see Photo 11.1). No more need to search through a bin to find a needle, at the risk of sticking yourself with it.
> **Cost:** Less than $2 per machine.

---

* Chapter 16 reports on the factory tours I took in Japan.

PHOTO 11.1   Velcro strip holding a needle case.

PHOTO 11.2   Cutting area before the installation of nylon bags.

Installation of a Scrap-Catching Bag

Problem: The synthetic fur is delivered in rolls, so the seamstress has to cut off a strip using scissors before being able to sew it. The scraps pile up on the floor at her feet (see Photo 11.2).

Solution: A nylon bag is placed under the roll of synthetic fur to catch the scraps (see Photo 11.3). To make the bags at low cost, we use our nylon leftovers.

Cost: Less than $10 per bag.

Designing Functional Packaging Tables

Problem: To package the final product, the employee needs a number of items set up all around her, including a pile of tissue paper folded in

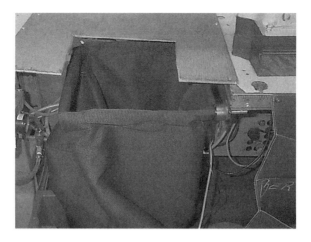

PHOTO 11.3 Cutting area is now always clean, thanks to the nylon bags.

PHOTO 11.4 Packing table where everything is within reach.

half on a small table, a roll of tape, and a number of cleaning products installed under the table or in a drawer.

Solution: A new packing table is designed; it includes everything the packager needs. A bar bolted to the front holds the pile of tissue paper, similar to a towel rack. On shelves, separators form boxes for tidy, handy storage of customer spec books, a spare roll of tape, and cleaning products (see Photo 11.4). The table is even equipped with a broom. Because packaging is the final operation the product goes through, we also install a sign that posts production in real time. At the end of each lot, the packager immediately records the style and quantity of boots produced. To reduce project implementation costs, we make these changes to the tables that we already have.

Cost: $50 per table.

PHOTO 11.5 Assembly station without a *talonnette* container (the *talonnettes* are the black pieces on the right side of the table).

Design of a Heel Reinforcement Container

Problem: The boots' felt lining includes a cloth layer to protect the heel area from repeated rubbing against the rubber base. These *talonnettes*, as we call them, are cut 64 layers of cloth at a time. The piles of *talonnettes* are then placed in a box and sent to the assembly station. During transport, the piles fall apart, and the employee who receives them wastes time finding them in the box and positioning them. As well, often, the *talonnettes* spread all over the table and fall to the floor. Once they're dirty, they're tossed in the garbage because it would cost more to clean them than just to make new ones.

Solution: Containers in the shape of *talonnettes* are designed (see Photo 11.5). The nylon cutter piles up the pieces as he cuts them. That way, they arrive at the assembly station in order and properly counted. The containers (Photo 11.6) become production *kanbans**.

Cost: $25 per container.

Creation of a Color Code for Bottom Injection and Transport

Problem: The rubber bottoms are injected in our Montreal factory, then shipped to the factories in Contrecoeur, New Hamburg, and Littleton. The injection machine has six stations such that bottoms in six different sizes can be injected at the same time. The operator who removes the bottoms from their molds sets them on a wheeled shelving unit to let them cool. The unit is then wheeled to the packaging station where the bottoms are placed in cardboard boxes according to their size. These

PHOTO 11.6 The *talonnette* container makes it possible to reduce wasted time and material losses.

boxes, identified with bar codes, are placed on a pallet and brought to shipping. The factories that receive these boxes often complain of packaging errors. For instance, they report the following problems:
- The sizes provided are not the ones indicated on the label (labeling error).
- The style of the bottoms in the box is not the one indicated on the label (labeling error).
- The boxes are incomplete (they contain fewer than 24 pairs of bottoms).
- The pairs of bottoms aren't properly matched (they include two right feet or two left feet).

We think that a lack of communication explains most of these errors. The Montreal factory employs people from 33 countries who speak 10 or more different languages. While French is the official working language in the factory, the communication difficulties between employees who speak different languages of course creates an obstacle to effective teamwork[*].

Solution: The six injection machine stations (see Photo 11.7) are painted in different colors: black, white, orange, yellow, red, and green. These same colors are also applied to the six shelves where the bottoms are cooled (see Photo 11.8). Self-stick labels in assorted colors are provided by a six-strip distributor to label the shipping boxes. Finally, the six stools set up to hold the boxes are also painted with the six colors (see Photo 11.10).

---

[*] Conscious of this reality, we offer French classes at the work site, and we encourage our non-Francophone employees to take them.

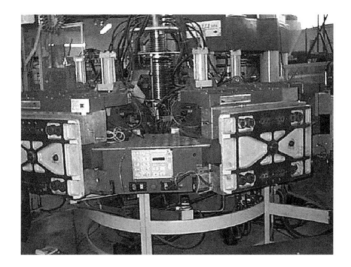

PHOTO 11.7 Injection machine with stations in six different colors.

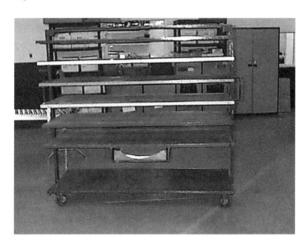

PHOTO 11.8 Wheeled unit with shelves in six different colors.

From now on, the operator just has to take a pair of bottoms from the red station, for example, and set it on the red shelf on the unit. Once the unit is taken to the packaging station, the employee who empties the red shelf makes sure to place its contents in the box that's set on the red stool, and stick on the label from the red distributor. And Bob's your uncle!

Because the color code is easy to understand, regardless of the language spoken by the manufacturing and packaging employees, far fewer errors are now reported in the factories receiving the bottoms!

Cost: Less than $100 for paint.

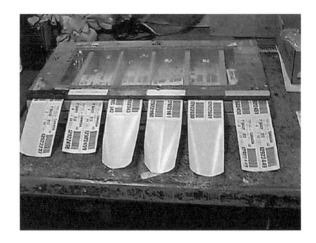

PHOTO 11.9 Distribution box with six different label colors.

PHOTO 11.10 Six stools in different colors. Color-based stock identification at every step of the process.

EXAMPLE OF A MEDIUM *KAIZEN*

Small *Kaizen* are not always enough to fix a problem.

Installation of a Box Lifting System

Problem: In our module-based production system, each member of our multidisciplinary team carries out the various tasks required to manufacture a product and prepare it for shipping, from A to Z. This means, among other things, that the boots' final labeling and packaging in a

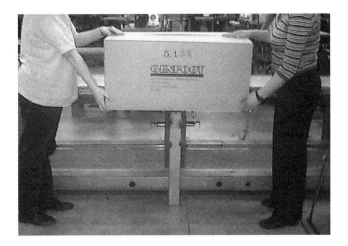

PHOTO 11.11 Manual lifting of a box of finished products.

cardboard box, and the transportation of this box to the conveyor, is all done by the team's seamstresses, taking turns*. Even if the packaging tables are placed as close as possible to the conveyor, the seamstresses need to lift the boxes to set them on it (see Photo 11.11). These boxes, which generally contain 12 pairs of boots, are fairly heavy, and all the more so when they're industrial boots with a steel bottom and steel toe.

The problem is even more serious for shorter employees, for whom lifting boxes weighing even just 10 or 12 kilograms can, in the long run, cause health problems such as tendonitis or bursitis.

When the first seamstresses complain about the situation, we try to reduce the weight of the boxes by suggesting that our customers receive boxes of 6 pairs instead of 12. But we still need to find a lasting solution to eliminate handling *muda** and *muri**.

Solution: I once faced a similar situation at Electrolux® in the early 1980s. As an industrial engineer, I had to redesign a workstation to make it more ergonomic. The problem was that an inspector had to lift a vacuum cleaner out of its box at the end of the production chain in order to do full quality control; but the machine weighed nearly 20 kilograms, and the tiny woman only weighed 45 kilograms herself! After watching the workstation for a half-day, I had a pretty good idea of what we needed to do. We had to move the inspection station closer to the production chain and install a mechanical arm to handle the vacuum cleaner as it was being inspected, as well as a half-moon-shaped conveyor and a moving platform that could return the vacuum cleaner to the chain after the tests.

---

* Previously, these activities were carried out by the packaging and finishing service; all the lifting was done by men who could regularly lift boxes weighing 15 or 20 kilograms without difficulty.

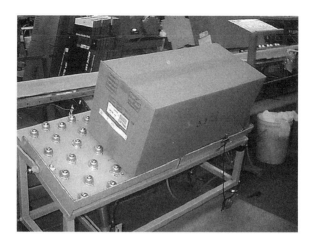

PHOTO 11.12 Box handling and lifting system.

Our module's problem isn't so different from that of the vacuum cleaner inspector. While I watch a packer at work, I ask a sewing machine mechanic to join me. Sylvain is really resourceful; there's nothing he can't do, and he's very good at his work. Whether I'm asking him to handle mechanics for sewing machines, welding, carpentry, plumbing, or electricity, I know he'll do a great job. I explain that I'd like to have a hydraulic or pneumatic lifting system to place boxes on the conveyer as it moves. The lifting table must also be suitable for packing.

A week later, Sylvain calls me to show me the new system he's made, which he's very proud of. He gives me a demonstration (see Photo 11.12).

The idea is very simple. The seamstress who's working on final packing sets an empty cardboard box on the smooth side of the lifting table. When the box is full, the packer closes it and pushes it to the other side of the table, which is set up with rolling balls. Next, the table tips and the box slides onto the conveyor. As well, Sylvain has taken things a step further than my idea. He called upon his creative genius. Instead of just a simple lifting mechanism as I'd suggested, he coupled one of the table's rolling balls with a detector that automatically sets off the table's tipping function toward the conveyor. Really smart! For a first try, I think his system is fantastic, and the employees of the module that tests it in production think it's extraordinary. After a few small tweaks and improvements, the handling system is standardized and we build one for every module (see Photo 11.13).

The goal of eliminating handling *muda* and the *muri* linked to the effort is reached.

Cost: About $1,000 per tipping table.

Savings in health and safety, and productivity gains: Some $100,000 per year.

PHOTO 11.13 The handling system in action.

EXAMPLE OF A BIG *KAIZEN*

Sometimes, it's worth it to take on bigger *Kaizen* to eliminate recurrent wastes of time and efficiency.

Automation of Strap Cutting and Gluing Tasks

Problem: On one of our products, the snowmobile boot, we have to attach vinyl straps to D-rings through which the laces must be threaded. There are 12 per pair for kids' sizes and 16 per pair for men's sizes.

The vinyl straps were cut on a press, and then sent to sewing. There, we had three worktables equipped with heaters on which bowls of hot glue were set. Four employees worked standing up around each table. The assembly method was as follows: the employee would pick up a cut vinyl strap, cover it with glue, pass it through the metal D-ring and close the two ends, after which the piece was ready to be sewn onto the nylon upper (see Photo 11.14). This task, which required no dexterity, attention, or effort, was often assigned to employees temporarily restricted to light work after a work accident, or dealing with postural or weightlifting limitations. You can imagine the boredom of repeating this maneuver more than 300 times an hour, 2,400 times a day, 12,000 times a week. Not the most enriching work. If there were such thing as a monotony *muda*, this activity would be a good example of it!

Because we assemble more than 5 million straps a year, the annual labor cost of this cutting and gluing operation was $250,000. The employees' pace was a lot slower than that of our automatic sewing machines, which sewed three to four rings in a single shot. So there was waiting *muda*. As well, we always need a minimum stock of straps for a day of production. If we add in

PHOTO 11.14 Employees manually assembling straps and D-rings.

the pieces of vinyl cut ahead of time for the straps, we could count more than 100,000 pieces of vinyl stored in the factory at any given time, so there was also stocking *muda*. We wanted to eliminate these waiting and stocking *mudas*.

> **Solution:** We set up an automation project so that we could get a machine to carry out the combined cutting and gluing operations for the straps, which would also save us quite a bit of money. With the help of an automation and robotics specialist, we designed a new machine, using the plan illustrated in Figure 11.1.
>
> The vinyl tape is mounted on a motorized unwinder that prevents the material from being stretched too much. The unwinder is equipped with a moving arm, making it possible to use wide-diameter rolls, which increases the machine's autonomy. A light detector signals that the machine is fully stocked with materials. The vinyl tape is guided by a precision slide toward a cutting station where a pneumatic press and

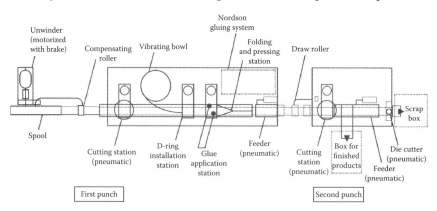

FIGURE 11.1 Diagram for the strap cutting and gluing machine, and its various stations.

PHOTO 11.15 Fully automated assembly chain.

a knife cut the front part of the strap. To minimize loss, the machine cuts two straps head-to-toe on a strip just barely wider than the strap. A vibrating bowl on two rails pushes the rings toward the next station. At the end of the rails, the rings are assembled with the straps. At the next station, the temperature-controlled hot glue is applied using a gun (a heated reservoir makes it possible to use glue chips, less expensive than the tube glue used previously). Then the pieces are guided toward a set of rollers that close the straps. A second press cuts the remainder of the strap. To ensure a precise process, rollers control the tension of the vinyl tape throughout the whole chain. At the end of the machine, the scraps are removed using a guillotine, while the good pieces are pushed toward a bin. The machine's minimum pace is a hundred pieces a minute (see Photo 11.15).

The machine is surrounded by safety barriers and its functions are controlled by a programmable controller. Orders are centralized to a control panel.

Manufacturing and implementation cost for the automated assembly chain: $75,000.

Savings: Over $240,000 per year.

EXAMPLE OF EVERYDAY *KAIZEN*

Of course, *Kaizen* is a great fit with the manufacturing industry but the philosophy that underpins it can be applied elsewhere, with results that are just as useful. Here's an illustration.

A few years ago, I undertook an exercise program to lose the 10 kilograms I'd put on over the years. One of the activities was fast walking on a treadmill. The first day of training, after 25 minutes at 5 kilometers per hour,

I was completely exhausted and on the verge of agony. Gradually, I increased the length of exercise time. By the end of just one week, I was doing 35 minutes at the same speed. This was nothing spectacular but it still represented a 40% improvement. By the end of the month, I could walk for an hour at a speed of 5 kilometers per hour without much effort whatsoever.

But, in the spirit of *Kaizen*, I couldn't stop there. I continued to increase my speed by 1 kilometer per hour per month while keeping the same time. I hit a plateau in the fourth month, when I reached a speed of 8 kilometers per hour. I couldn't go faster without running. So I decided to maintain my speed but increase the exercise time by 10 minutes. I hit a second plateau at the sixth month, when I started to find the exercise long and monotonous. I noticed then that I no longer had to start at a low speed for the first 5 minutes, so I could walk at 8 kilometers per hour from the get-go.

At that point, I'd surpassed my weight loss goal by a kilogram. Proud of my results, I stopped my program. And in so doing, I abandoned my *Kaizen*.

A few months later, I'd gained back a few kilograms and had to start training again. To my great despair, the day I started exercising again, I was worn out after half an hour at 5 kilometers per hour! I understood then that even after I'd reached my goal, I should have continued to stay motivated and avoid falling back into my bad habits, or at least I should have maintained my new weight. By failing to progress, I slid backward. *Kaizen,* with its progress in small steps, proved itself relevant even in my personal life!

Progressive, continual improvement has also proved its worth in competition sports. This philosophy is at the root of lower and lower times clocked in swimming and running competitions, for instance. And these efforts boost the level of competition from one championship to the next.

This is the vision that *Kaizen* rests upon: tomorrow's goal is to surpass today's standard.

Chapter 12

Tour of a Chinese Supplier: A Wake-Up Call

EARLY 1998

In early 1998, I have to travel to China to visit one of our hiking shoe suppliers. This type of item requires a large amount of labor; no major North American factory is able to produce them at a competitive rate. Nike®, Reebok®, and Adidas® brand shoes are all manufactured in the Far East, mainly in China.

I want to state something up front. Many articles have discredited these Chinese factories, saying that they employ young children and abuse their workers. Alerted by what they've read, many of our customers even asked us, earlier in the year to commit in writing that we won't tolerate such practices among our suppliers. On my part, I know that we're doing business with the most highly reputed Chinese companies in the industry, which supply the market's best international companies, and that the reality is more nuanced.

MORE THAN A COMPANY: A CITY!

I've already toured many world-class factories in the United States, Europe, Taiwan, and Korea. But this trip is my first one to China. I'm looking forward to touring this shoe company, which employs more than 16,000 workers in its factories.

A vehicle comes to pick me up at the hotel and we drive for a solid hour past the typical scenery of tiny villages. The car finally stops in front of a giant fence, where I'm greeted. After we introduce ourselves, the doors open onto an agglomeration that I'd describe as being more like a city than a village; in fact, it's our supplier's city (see Photo 12.1). All their workers live here.

PHOTO 12.1 Life in this factory complex is like that of a small city.

Some 30 apartment buildings, where the workers live, line an asphalt road. We also pass a cafeteria, a training center, a gym, and a disco. It's quite impressive!

Our Chinese supplier is a vertically integrated company. It even manufactures its own rubber, which it transforms into soles of all colors. The factories I tour are impeccable, and the machines are very well maintained and mostly very recent.

Each of the company's multifloor factories specializes in one manufacturing process. They each have an adjacent dormitory that holds 1,000 people.

WORKERS IN RESIDENCE

The seamstresses employed by the company must be at least 16 years old. They are, for the most part, recruited from nearby rural areas but some of them come from as far as 300 miles away. The young girls' parents are very proud that they've been recruited because with their work they provide valuable financial help to their families. As well, they're learning a trade that could help the girls when they retire (the year they get married, around age 25).

Starting their first day of work, the young girls are greeted by people in uniform who teach them the basic rules (see Photo 12.2). Then they're paired up with their dormitory mates. They're submitted to strict discipline similar to that of a regiment. They work six days a week, up to 12 hours a day*.

But these factories don't simply reap the benefits of having "captive" workers. Balancing the flow of orders is a major challenge. For instance,

---

* During my tour, I learned that Nike, one of the factory's major customers, had imposed a limit of 72 hours of work per week after being targeted by a media campaign.

PHOTO 12.2 New workers receive their first instructions.

if the production of a certain model requires 100 workers, but the next one is less complex and requires only 75, what do you do with the 25 excess workers? In North America, temporary layoff is a standard solution in such cases; but in Chinese factories, that's impossible. And with good reason. The young girls, who are housed and fed by the employer, may come from very far away. Sending them home would cost the company too much, so it has to keep them and find them something to do in the factory, even if there's a labor surplus. This explains the presence of a high number of assembly line inspectors. They're easy to tell apart from the others because they wear a colored armband. On some chains, there are almost as many inspectors as workers!

REALM OF *MUDA**

The factory's sewing sections are particularly clean and organized. But while most of the sewing machines are new, they're not equipped with any additional automation mechanisms. By comparison, in Genfoot's factories, all the sewing machines are equipped with thread-cutters and automatic foot lifts, as well as small computers that count the stitches, regulate the thread's tension, and so forth; they save us precious seconds of assembly work. In China, adding these options doesn't make sense because the cost of labor is minimal compared to the investment that would be required to automate the machines; so the Chinese companies don't bother.

The sewing areas' layout is traditional (see Photo 12.3). Seamstresses, seated in front of their machines, each perform just one operation at a time. They work at a very good pace and seem focused on their work. They don't

PHOTO 12.3 Sewing section of one of the Chinese factories I toured.

even raise their eyes to watch us walk by! The area is a copy of our Contrecoeur factory *before* we implemented just in time* and module-based work.

I see nothing reprehensible or worrisome apart from overproduction, waiting, and stocking *mudas*. Really, although an army (it must be said) of workers is working at a fast pace in the factory, I can easily identify *mudas* everywhere I look. The seven kinds of *mudas* are all represented, and I think if there were more than seven, you could find the extras here too! Knowing that I'm in one of the biggest and best shoe factories in the world, I'm perplexed at all this. So I decide to take a closer look by following the trajectory of one of our products from A to Z, from one floor to the next, from operation to operation. I slow down to watch several operations that add absolutely no value to our product. In some cases, I'd even call them useless.

The most flagrant case is that of four workers seated around a table to inspect the little plastic pieces that feature our logo. We produce these pieces ourselves and deliver them to our subcontractors packaged in bags of 2,000. Around the table, two girls seem to be counting them, one by one. They then place them before two other workers, who glance at them and put them back in their bags.

To be sure that I understand, I ask a supervisor who's serving as an interpreter during the conversation, what the first two workers are doing:

"They're counting the pieces."
"Have there ever been some missing?"
"No, there are never any missing."
"What are the other two workers doing?"

"They're doing a visual inspection."
"Have they ever rejected a piece?"
"No."

The worst thing about all this is that before we ship the bags, we determine exactly how many pieces are in them because we weigh them with an electronic scale!

One of the workers then says something in Chinese, pointing to another supervisor, who approaches with a decisive step. A short discussion ensues. My interpreter whispers that I shouldn't push the issue and that he'll explain later what it's all about. When we're further away, he tells me that the workers are given redundant work to do, but are told that it's useful to keep them busy when there's less work to do.

In total, 254 different people touch our hiking shoes during the manufacturing process. Of this number, there might be 60 at most who add value to them. If we transposed this situation to our factories, we'd go bankrupt for sure!

When I tally up my observations, I'm concerned at the idea that our supplier is billing us for all this wasted time.

Another observation: while the work conditions in the factory are very good on the whole, I nevertheless note a few operations that would be considered unacceptable in our factories. For example, a huge number of workers, using brushes, must glue all the parts that come to them without the benefit of adequate ventilation, and others work crouched on stools to remove uppers from their lasts, putting their backs at risk.

QUALITY, BUT AT THE EXPENSE OF PRODUCTIVITY

What hits me the most is the quality of the items produced in the Chinese factories I tour. Not that long ago, China had a reputation for producing low-end, poor-quality items, but that's clearly no longer the case—at least not with our supplier. But unlike their Japanese counterparts, the Chinese companies assign a very high number of inspectors to every step of production. Quality happens because of overquality. This excessive inspection would be considered *muda* in Japan, where they work instead to eliminate problems at the source using *jidoka** and *poka-yoke**. Considering the wage disparity between the two countries, if Toyota assigned this many workers to assembly, a Corolla would cost as much as a Rolls Royce.

DIFFICULT NEW AWARENESS

During my long flight home, I can't help but think about everything I just saw. The images of the thousands of workers producing shoes and boots scare me. The factory I just toured has more workers than the population of all three cities where we operate Genfoot factories! How can you compete with such a giant? How much will we have to improve our productivity to compete with this kind of adversary, when our seamstresses earn 10 times more than theirs do? How, in this context, can North American companies justify the necessary investments to keep their local factories open? Can we be competitive without doing so on the backs of our workers, without asking them to make enormous concessions? How will this David-and-Goliath duel end?

UNEQUAL STRUGGLE

I come back from my tour of the Chinese factories feeling worried. Fifteen years later, I'm still worried, because China has become one of the greatest world powers in the field of manufacturing. To understand, you just have to look at a few numbers that bear witness to an economic situation that's more and more favorable to Chinese industry:

- The number of jobs in the Chinese manufacturing sector increased by 13.1 million between 2002 and 2009, which represents 15% growth[*].
- Despite a few adjustments, Chinese currency, or the renminbi (or yuan), was consistently undervalued in 2013[†]. While the Chinese government allowed the currency to float within a narrow margin in 2005 and increased the margin in 2012, the variation in the exchange rate is still very limited[‡].
- In 2008, with an average hourly wage of US$1.36, Chinese manufacturing workers received less than 4% of the hourly wage of their American counterparts[§]! According to the World Bank, from 2000 to 2012, the growth of China's gross domestic product was 10.6%, while it was 2.7% for the rest of the world and 1.9% and 1.7% for Canada and the United States, respectively[¶].

---

[*] Banister, Judith (US Department of Labor – Bureau of Labor Statistics). 2013. "China's manufacturing employment and hourly labor compensation, 2002–2009." www.bls.gov, June 7, 2013. [Online] www.bls.gov/fls/china_method.pdf. Accessed February 21, 2014.

[†] Katz, Ian and Klimasinska, Kasia. 2013. "U.S. Treasury says yuan hasn't appreciated as much as needed." www.bloomberg.com, October 30, 2013. [Online] www.bloomberg.com/news/2013-10-30/u-s-treasury-says-yuan-hasn-t-appreciated-as-much-as-needed-1-.html. Accessed February 21, 2014.

[‡] Reuters. 2012. "Timeline: China's reforms of yuan exchange rate." www.reuters.com, April 14, 2012. [Online] www.reuters.com/article/2012/04/14/us-china-yuan-timeline-idUSBRE83D03820120414. Accessed February 21, 2014.

[§] Banister, Judith and Cook, George (US Department of Labor – Bureau of Labor Statistics). 2013. "China's manufacturing employment and hourly labor compensation, 2002–2009." *Monthly Labor Review*, March 2011. [Online] http://www.bls.gov/opub/mlr/2011/03/art4full.pdf. Accessed February 21, 2014.

[¶] World Bank. 2013. "2013 Economy – 4.1 World Development Indicators: Growth of Output." worldbank.org. [Online] wdi.worldbank.org/table/4.1. Accessed February 21, 2014.

In the 2000s, the United States lost 5.7 million manufacturing jobs (meaning 33% of jobs in the field). This deindustrialization was worse than the one we experienced during the 1980s and the Great Depression[*]! According to the Economic Policy Institute in Washington, DC, over a third of job losses in the American manufacturing sector between 2001 and 2011 are attributable to China[†].

And for the North American shoe industry in particular, the situation is hardly reassuring:

- In 2008, the Canadian shoe industry employed only 2,300 people (between 2004 and 2008 alone, jobs dropped in the sector by 39.5%). That same year, more than 90% of the Canadian shoe market (CAN$1.8 billion) was held by imported products, of which nearly 70% came from China (CAN$1.2 billion)[‡].
- In 2010, China alone produced 12.6 billion pairs of shoes, or 62% of the world's production. Three quarters of American shoe imports came from China, for a value of US$16.4 billion[§].
- In 2011, although a million American workers were employed in the local shoe industry, 98.6% of shoes sold in the United States came from abroad[¶].

---

[*] Atkinson, Robert. 2013. "Why the 2000s were a lost decade for American manufacturing." www.industryweek.com, March 14, 2013. [Online] www.industryweek.com/global-economy/why-2000s-were-lost-decade-american-manufacturing. Accessed February 21, 2014.
[†] Kurtzleben, Danielle. 2012. "Report: America lost 2.7 million jobs to China in 10 years." www.usnews.com, August 24, 2012. [Online] www.usnews.com/news/articles/2012/08/24/report-america-lost-27-million-jobs-to-china-in-10-years. Accessed February 21, 2014.
[‡] Industry Canada. 2011. "Footwear industry profile." www.ic.gc.ca, November 29, 2011. [Online] www.ic.gc.ca/eic/site/026.nsf/eng/h_00072.html. Accessed February 21, 2014.
[§] World Footwear. 2011. "World footwear – 2011 yearbook." www.worldfootwear.com, September 2011. [Online] www.apiccaps.pt/c/document_library/get_file?uuid=7200889f-26e8-4329-855d-5bdb268eb49a&groupId=10136. Accessed February 21, 2014.
[¶] American Apparel & Footwear Association (AAFA). 2012. "AAFA releases ShoeStats 2012 report." www.wewear.org, September 24, 2012. [Online] www.wewear.org/aafa-releases-shoestats-2012-report. Accessed February 22, 2014.

Chapter 13

End of an Era

2003

Ten years have passed since the Contrecoeur factory's transformation, and we've hit a nice cruising speed. But globalization and the market's evolution have changed our situation so much that we need to restructure our operations and re-evaluate our options. And now we're backed into a terrible corner.

INCREASINGLY FIERCE GLOBAL COMPETITION

For several years now, the North American footwear industry has been facing a creeping threat as a result of market globalization: dumping*. Chinese-made shoes and boots are flooding store shelves, and are often sold at such low prices that they don't even cover the costs of the raw materials! For instance, negotiators can stock up on Chinese-made children's rain boots for $1.99 a pair, while the materials alone to make those same boots would cost us more than $2.50. This insidious competition is having devastating effects on local shoe and boot manufacturers: while they haven't all closed shop, our North American competitors have all given up on local manufacturing and are sourcing 100% from China, Vietnam, or other developing countries that offer qualified labor at a low price.

Because of this situation, we've undertaken steps, through the Shoe Manufacturers' Association of Canada, with the Canadian International Trade Tribunal to have it put an end to such disloyal practices. We presented the Tribunal with Chinese products sold in our stores at prices lower than what the raw materials cost. When it finished its investigation, the Tribunal agreed with us in that it recognized the existence of dumping but then, on January 22, 2003, they published the following decision:

"The Canadian International Trade Tribunal [...] hereby finds that the dumping [in Canada] of certain waterproof footwear [...] constructed wholly or in part of rubber or plastic, [...] originating in or exported from [...] Macao, China [...] has not caused material injury and is not threatening to cause material injury to the domestic industry."

—Inquiry No. NQ-2002-002*

In other words: Yes, we recognize that disloyal practices exist, but because you're working in a small production branch that doesn't employ too many people, you're on your own!

The Tribunal's decision hurts Genfoot pretty badly. The noose is tightening on the Contrecoeur factory, which is starting to lose orders.

The paradox is that even if we were very productive, our products are no longer competitive when compared to our competitors' dumped products.

FACTORY THAT IS PRODUCTIVE, BUT UNDERUSED

Until now, the Contrecoeur factory has been moving along at a great clip. All our employees are multidisciplinary and efficient. Our productivity is at its strongest. For the first time, the factory's overall efficiency is hitting 94%. We've just improved our productivity ratio by 10% compared to the previous year, which represents $0.3346 per minute; it's our best in 10 years. These results are bringing in new productivity increases of more than $100,000.

But despite everything, the situation is far from being ideal. One of the problems that has persisted for decades at the factory is that we manufacture a seasonal product: winter boots. Because of this seasonal character, the factory only produces for eight months of the year. Orders start to arrive in February and March. But because with our new pull production* system, we only produce to order; manufacturing starts in March and ends in December, when the last orders are delivered. Normally, children's boot orders must be delivered first, in early August just before the school year begins. Adult products are delivered later in the season.

During the slow season, between December and March, production employees are laid off and take advantage of the opportunity to rest and spend the winter at home. But the maintenance, supervision, and management teams remain at work. Some teams use the slow time to complete their preventive maintenance projects or renovate workstations. Others prepare samples for the coming season. This work involves the design, cutting, and sewing departments. Our few office employees prepare new spec sheets and estimate new production costs.

During this time, the atmosphere is pretty relaxed, and the stress level is at its lowest. And, between you and me, I can admit that all the work that's

* Available at www.citt.gc.ca/dumping/inquirie/findings/archive_nq2c002_e.asp#P9_477. Accessed February 2014.

done in the slow season could be done in a single month. But it's unthinkable for us to periodically lay off the qualified people of the winter team, because they'd quickly go get a permanent year-round job elsewhere.

CHANGING FASHION

For the second year in a row, sales for the boot models produced at Contrecœur (big, warm boots for outdoor activities) have dropped sharply. The fashion is now turning toward lighter boots, which are less cumbersome and not as warm but which can also be worn in everyday settings. Adults are no longer wearing logger boots and snowmobile boots; orders for this type of product have fallen by half in the past decade and, as a result, so has the number of employees at our factory.

CONFLATION OF CIRCUMSTANCE

At this time, one of our biggest competitors declares bankruptcy. The Kaufman Footwear company, which has been making Sorel boots since 1908 in Ontario, has to forfeit after posting major financial losses for the second consecutive year. This closely held family company bears a strong resemblance to ours, in terms of both product range and quality; we often fight over the same customers. However, there's one major difference between us: the Kaufman company is still working with a push production model. The final nail in the company's coffin is that last winter was particularly mild and not very snowy, so boot sales were much lower than usual. Because the company bases its production on forecasts, it was stuck with a huge stock of unsold products. The merchandise had to be liquidated at a discount, which is never good for a company's finances or for its brand reputation. While we often say that we learn from our mistakes, unfortunately that wasn't the case with Kaufman. The company made the same mistake the next year, once again producing a large stock of boots in hopes of better sales. Bad luck hit once more, because the next winter was no colder or snowier than the previous one, with the same result: Kaufman was stuck with millions of dollars in unsold products. That's when its creditors lost patience and claimed their due, thus sealing the company's fate.

Because Kaufman and Genfoot deal with the same bankers, they (the bankers) contact us to find out if we are interested in the bankrupt factory's facilities, equipment, tools, or brand name. The Cook family and I make a trip to visit the company owners and see their factory. As soon as I step in the door, I shiver. I see the Contrecoeur factory, pre-transformation, all over again. Long conveyors loaded with products. Piles of unfinished boots scattered all over the floor. Wheeled dollies. A leather cutting section in a closed-off corner. Stock, stock, and more stock. I find the spectacle depressing.

But it hits me, also, that 500 qualified, experienced employees, after working until just recently in this building, are suddenly jobless.

Our felt factory in New Hamburg is located less than 20 kilometers from the Kaufman factory, so the former employees file through our offices day after day, hoping to find work. We aren't hiring, but considering the sudden availability of these experienced workers, I have the idea that we could study the possibility of converting our felt factory into a production center for finished felt linings. We'd have to take the rolls of freshly needle-punched felt*, cut them, and sew them in order to provide our assembly factories with a ready-to-use component.

After a few weeks of study, it becomes clear that not only is the project viable, but it would also save us over $100,000 a year. The experienced seamstresses from the Kaufman factory who we'd hire would cost us less than the ones at Contrecoeur, and we'd save enormous handling and transportation fees by carrying out all the felt-making operations on-site. As well, the New Hamburg factory could be converted quickly, in a single season, without requiring a long production break or major expenses.

Unfortunately, the flip side of the coin is that transferring the cutting and sewing of nearly 1.5 million felt linings to New Hamburg would lead to the loss of some six weeks of work for 30 or so employees at Contrecoeur. This production migration would be fatal for a factory already suffering the effects of underproduction. If we carried out this plan, the Contrecoeur factory would have fewer than 130 permanent employees and they'd work only six months of the year; the overhead for keeping the factory in operation would become exorbitant, considering its production, and thus difficult to justify.

INESCAPABLE SITUATION

Faced with the reality of a market flooded with dumped products, a dramatic drop in orders, seasonal production, high overhead costs, changing fashion trends, and a 100+ year-old building starting to show its age, I have to face the facts: the Contrecoeur factory can't survive without imperiling Genfoot's financial health. I have a difficult time accepting the situation. I can't believe that the most productive shoe factory in North America is so ill-fated! Over the years, we've succeeded in training our employees like no other company has. They're devoted, experienced, and versatile but we have no more work to offer them!

Hard Decision

For a moment, I think about moving one or two injection machines from the Montreal factory to the Contrecoeur factory; the transfer would make it

---

* Felt needle punching is a process by which the polyester fibers that make up the felt are punched through from all sides, at high speed, by more than 10,000 needles in order to mix them together.

possible to produce an additional item for spring and fall, which would save the jobs of 30 or so employees during the slow season. Unfortunately, upon consideration, the idea turns out to be unreasonable. Injection machines must be operated by highly specialized workers who we're unlikely to find in or near a small town like Contrecoeur; truly, this type of worker is even difficult to recruit in a big city like Montreal, because the plastics industry is doing so well that it's suffering from a serious labor shortage.

I think about another option. Because we freed up nearly 10,000 square feet in our Montreal injection plant by moving the head-office workspaces into our Lachine distribution center building, I consider using the space for all the remaining boot production—the boots currently sewn at the Contrecoeur factory. This way, we could offer all the Contrecoeur workers a job in Montreal, if they want one.

The only positive point for Genfoot in this dark picture is that our three other factories could easily absorb the production of finished products.

Armed with this scenario, I call a meeting with the company's senior managers to present my closure project for our Contrecoeur flagship factory, with the production transfer as a result. It's mid-December and everyone's just thinking about the Christmas holidays. But the thing that bothers me the most is the fate awaiting the Contrecoeur factory employees. Will they agree to follow production to Montreal? And what will happen to the ones who don't come along?

After laying out the rather depressing picture of the current situation at the Contrecoeur factory, I present the executive with my plan to transfer sewing operations from Contrecoeur to Montreal and to restructure the company.

The decision is unanimous: we need to close the Contrecoeur factory as soon as possible. Keeping the factory open for longer would only postpone the inevitable without bringing any real comfort to the employees. But transferring production to another one of our factories would have the immediate effect of making us yet more productive and competitive, without increasing our manufacturing overhead. So the question isn't "Why does the factory have to close?" but rather "When can we do it?"

Painful Delay

Starting with this meeting and the executives' decision, I feel the weight of the world on my shoulders. I have to decide on the date we'll announce the closure to the employees as well as the date of the last day of production. I also have to find out from government authorities about the appropriate procedures to follow. Legally speaking, we have to give the employees at least eight weeks' notice of the closure and plan to pay out major amounts in severance packages.

Two weeks before Christmas and a week away from our traditional holiday party, I realize that I've chosen a very bad time to announce a closure to the factory workers. So I decide to wait until after the holidays, in January, to bring the employees together and tell them about the unfortunate news*.

As the end-of-year holidays approach, the employees are all in a good mood as they get ready for the Christmas party. The big party, organized by the social club, is an employee favorite, and people rarely miss it.

As well, this year's party is particularly special because we're taking the opportunity to pay tribute to Monique, the factory manager, who's retiring. Monique is part of the third generation in her family to work at the Contrecoeur factory; she's given more than half her life to it.

To thank her, I prepare an audiovisual PowerPoint™ presentation about her, which I show to all the employees on the night of the party before giving her a set of golf clubs as a retirement gift. To help me put together my presentation, I ask Monique's kids to send me a few funny photos of her on skates, playing golf, practicing archery, and skiing. With the help of one of our designers, I alter a few photos to show her as Tiger Woods' golf partner or as hockey teammates with Wayne Gretzky. I really can't wait to thank this dynamic, unique woman, who has been the factory's soul. Without her conviction and determination to see our project succeed, we'd still be at square one, trying to figure out where to start.

During the celebration, however, I am very uneasy sitting in the middle of some hundred employees who are only thinking about the party. My heart is heavy as I watch them dance and sing. Being the only one to know what the near future has in store for them, I feel guilty of a crime I didn't commit. I would so much have wanted to share the decision with Monique and get it off my chest, but it was unthinkable to deal her that sort of blow under the circumstances. So I decide not to talk to anyone about it, to avoid spreading the news; Contrecoeur is a very small town, and news gets around fast. I cheer up myself by telling myself I can't do anything to change the situation. The key factors are out of my control. And the decision to close the Contrecoeur factory, while very hard to make, will help the company be more competitive with its three other factories, and ensure a solid future for some time to come, which saves jobs as a result.

Closure Announcement

On the morning of January 5, 2004, I call Monique at her home and ask how she spent the holidays. I then ask if I can come by for a visit. From the tone of my voice, she knows something's wrong. Also, for 13 years now, although we know each other well, I've never called her at home. So right away, she says,

---

* Some later reproached me for not informing them earlier. It's true that on the one hand, if they'd known they'd soon be jobless, they may have spent less on gifts or put less on credit. I had thought of this. But the other option would have been difficult too. The idea of ruining Christmas for more than 100 families and their kids wouldn't have made me feel any better. Who wants to be the Scrooge who spoils his employees' Christmas? One way or the other, I had to learn to live with my decision.

"You want to tell me that you're closing the factory?" When I confirm, to my great relief, she says she wants to be there with me when I make the announcement to the employees, although she's now retired.

We meet at the factory an hour after my call, and we ask all the employees to come to a meeting in front of the "communications bridge." When I see the whole group gathered, I think surely they've guessed what I'm about to announce. Monique's presence at my side, when she has officially left the factory, isn't terribly reassuring to them. Nervously, I tell them about all the obstacles the factory is facing: seasonal production, loss of orders, climate changes and demand for boots that aren't as warm, disloyal competition and product dumping*, upper production moved to Asia†, and felt manufacturing moved to our New Hamburg factory.

The crowd is filled with long faces, and murmurs start to spread, when a loud voice cries out, "So you're going to close the factory?" I haven't finished laying the groundwork for the conclusion but I have to answer yes. The minutes that follow seem to last an eternity. Everyone's talking and yelling at once. I hear a few invectives from the back of the room, as well as wailing and crying. It's the kind of situation nobody ever wants to experience. It's only when Monique starts talking that the employees calm down. She takes to task the ones who have insulted me, and she stands in my defense. She explains that they can't blame me for circumstances that are out of my control. Taken together, the changing market for winter boots and outdoor boots, the seasonal nature of our production, and the dumping of Chinese products have combined to force the factory's closure. The Cook family and Joe Bichai aren't responsible for all this.

I begin to speak again. I insist on the importance of what we've accomplished together. The Contrecoeur factory is, and always will be, cited as an example of a successful Lean* transformation. Everything we've accomplished will serve as an example in our other factories. I explain that there are still some 400,000 pairs of boots to produce each year, and that they'll be sewn in Montreal. At the same time, I offer a job at our Montreal factory to any employee who wants one. For those who are interested in the transfer but for whom the travel is a problem, I even offer to set up private bus transportation between Contrecoeur and a Montreal metro station‡. For those who don't want to take us up on the transfer offer, I let them know that a reassignment committee will be created to help them find work. I also tell them that

---

* As a result, we need to lay off people more and more regularly. The factory gradually empties, and the overhead starts to become a burden. Because we can't boost production, we need to reduce staff.

† Toward the early 2000s, we have to resolve to get our boot upper supplies in China. This is the component that requires the most labor. And when it comes to embroidery, appliqués, laces, and other elements of uppers, the Contrecoeur factory can't stay competitive because of labor costs. When we make this decision, the factory loses the production of slightly more than a million uppers and some four to six weeks of annual production.

‡ To our great surprise, none of the factory's workers take us up on our transfer offer. Only our engineer, Nadine, accepts a Montreal assignment.

we'll have a severance package program based on seniority. I let the workers know that the factory will continue to operate until February 27, for eight additional weeks.

Final Weeks

While the past eight weeks of production at the Contrecoeur factory tick away, there's no time to lose. This period goes by lightning-fast for me because I'm busy negotiating the severance package plan with the factory committee, starting up the reassignment committee, and finalizing the equipment inventory that must be transferred or sold. During this time, production goes on at a stunningly normal pace; despite the many problems and dramas the employees are going through due to the closure, they are determined to preserve their reputation and show us their pride in doing good work until the very end.

As well, we have to prepare to kick off a new sewing department in Montreal. It will benefit from all the positive and negative experiences of the modular production we tested at the Contrecoeur factory. From now on, hand-to-hand and versatility will be obligatory. The seamstresses will be trained to carry out all the boot assembly tasks from A to Z.

Despite this period of intense activity, I have a really difficult time with the Contrecoeur factory closure, to the point that my health begins to suffer. After losing 20 pounds and experiencing constant chest pain, I have to see a doctor. When my electrocardiogram comes back normal, the doctor explains that my symptoms are the effect of the intense stress I'm experiencing. It takes me months to feel better.

AFTER CONTRECOEUR: LEAN AT WORK

The Contrecoeur factory closure didn't mark the end of Genfoot's JIT*/Lean adventure. Quite the opposite. We pursued our process in our other factories, and perfected our operating methods. Not only have we stayed the course despite the effects of globalization and succeeded in saving our workers' jobs, but we're also more productive, competitive, and profitable today than we were in the Contrecoeur era. And I'm proud to say that our three factories are currently working at full capacity, to the point that we're discussing expansion projects for our North American facilities!

The assembly of a sewn boot is now greatly simplified. The upper, which required several sewing operations, is now bought as a finished product. The felt lining, which required three different sewing operations, is now cut and sewn in our Ontario factory. As before, the rubber base (bottom) is produced in the Montreal factory. We only need to take care of individual or bulk packaging using boxes, tissue paper, price tags, stickers, and hang tags.

PHOTO 13.1 Pre-prepared pallet of components required for producing lots.

Because each pair of boots is sewn, assembled, and packaged by a single person, all the operations without added value that were still around have now been eliminated.

From now on, pallets holding all the components needed for finishing each lot of boots are prepared at the triage station at the distribution center. The pallets, which also serve as *kanban**, contain all the materials required for four hours of work (see Photo 13.1). A single handler (the *mizusumachi**) supplies the modules with base materials twice a day.

The sewing department, installed on the same floor in the space formerly occupied by offices, is equipped with a service elevator to facilitate handling.

Order management is automated; it's based on the sequence of orders and the delivery dates that must be met. Our IT (information technology) system manages lot production and sends the order preparation sequence, not to production but to the distribution center. Because the tag on each box of finished products is numbered, the box can be tracked in real time by the customer service department; they can also keep the customers informed about the progress of their orders, easily and at any time.

Finally, by mutual agreement, the company's employees and management chose to end the productivity gain-sharing plan and replace it with a regular profit-sharing plan. The same bonus system is used in all three factories, the two distribution centers, and the head office.

Chapter 14

Winning Conditions for a Successful JIT and *Kaizen* Implementation Project

MARCH 1993

UNCONDITIONAL COMMITMENT FROM SENIOR MANAGEMENT

It's clear that to institute a major change in strategy or organizational culture, the company's senior management must be on board. In a JIT* context, where all the employees' work habits need to change, the bar is set even higher. What's needed is unconditional commitment on the part of senior management because while the result is well worth the effort, the process can be arduous. And I can't insist strongly enough on the importance of the process.

I could compare the process of Lean*/JIT and *Kaizen** implementation at our factory to that of a person who has never practiced a sport and is in bad physical shape, and who's asked to represent his country at the next Olympic triathlon four years from now. They'd have to be disciplined, get a good coach, train hard, and invest blood, sweat, and tears to get there. The path is long and strewn with obstacles, so the athlete-to-be would need to be motivated and convinced that he could reach his goal. But how could he stay the course if the people supervising him doubted whether the experiment would succeed?

Let's go back to the moment when Genfoot began its "training." It's early March 1993. The equipment is in place, the employees are trained, and the accumulated orders are waiting to be filled. This is the official beginning of our company's new era. The system to ensure our survival is in place, and the whole organization is fully ready...or so we think. But the first week of operation is more chaotic than expected. The foremen are soon at a loss for what to do. The employees seem to have forgotten all the concepts they learned in training. The factory's productivity barely hits 50%. Tensions among the seamstresses are at an all-time high. The customers are getting impatient. Total crisis! Meanwhile, the 5% of employees who were grumbling against the new system are strutting around the factory with big smiles, happy to see that this turn of events seems to mean they were right, while we, the management, are encouraging everyone and strengthening our presence in the factory to help motivate the other 95%.

Without steely determination, the situation would discourage pretty much any company management! But it's precisely in this kind of context that their indefatigable commitment is essential.

*****

The following anecdote reveals Genfoot senior management's attitude toward the change undertaken at the Contrecoeur factory.

It's March 4, 1993, at 8 a.m. My boss stops by my office and after we exchange greetings, he presents me with his *Wall Street Journal*. The big headline on the Economy page reads: "Allen-Edmonds Shoe Tries 'Just-in-Time' Production – But Company Painfully Finds Approach Isn't Perfect Fit for Small Concerns" (see Photo 14.1).

Whoa! Shivers run through my body. This is an international shoe company like ours that tried to implement JIT, failed, and decided to go back to piecework, stock, a production line setup, and so forth after losing a million dollars. What a catastrophe! For the first time, I feel doubt. I'm worried. Have I acted too quickly? Maybe I should have waited at least another season to become more familiar with the industry, which I still didn't know too well, before launching the company into the Lean adventure. Maybe we should have proceeded section by section instead of all at once...

I've never heard of the company in question; really, I thought we were the first in the industry to try implementing JIT. I feel my tension rise with every line of the article I read. During this whole time, my president remains standing in front of me, waiting for me to comment. Faced with my silence and my troubled look, he says to me, "Do you know what their problem is?"

After thinking for a few seconds, I answer: "First, I see no mention of employee training. Second, it seems that the change was rushed: you shouldn't try to put a just-in-time system into place without planning the transition and the culture change. You can't just impose it on the employees. JIT isn't a system you install; it's a management philosophy that requires that you think in JIT terms for all your activities. Really, it's a lifestyle!"

I quickly reread the article, and I add that you can't simply eliminate a piecework bonus system, even if it's terrible, without replacing it with some other form of reward—which Allen-Edmonds Shoe didn't do. By eliminating piecework like this, they dipped into the employees' wallets.

"You know, Joe," replies Gordon, "I don't know this company any more than you do, but I'm totally in agreement with you on the importance of

ENTERPRISE

Allen-Edmonds Shoe Tries 'Just-in-Time' Production

But Company Painfully Finds Approach Isn't Perfect Fit for Small Concerns

By BARBARA MARSH
Staff Reporter of THE WALL STREET JOURNAL

Just-in-time production practices can work wonders for big companies by improving efficiency. But many small firms are still struggling to reap the benefits.

Consider Allen-Edmonds Shoe Corp. a 71-year-old maker of pricey shoes. Three years ago, the Port Washington, Wis., company tried just-in-time methods to speed production, boost customer satisfaction and save money. The result? "It really flopped miserably," says John Stollenwerk, the company's president and biggest shareholder. The manufacturer lost $1 million on the project — and in 1991, resumed doing some things the old way.

Widespread In Japan

Just-in-time practices widespread in Japan and increasingly popular in the U.S., promise to reduce a company's inventory investment and slash production time. Among other things, the just-in-time approach calls for supplying work stations with the precise amount of material needed at the exact time required, thereby eliminating a manufacturer's warehousing of raw materials.

Large companies that dedicate workers and machines to producing items in huge volumes generally derive the greatest efficiencies from just-in-time methods, technology experts say. But small companies with short runs of a variety of products often fail to make such gains. Allen-Edmonds, for instance, makes 41,000 variations of men's and women's shoes in many styles, colors and sizes, and mostly in limited runs. So, the company must keep switching product lines, thereby reducing efficiency.

"It's somewhat difficult for a small company to achieve some of the just-in-time gains of large companies," says Thomas W. Bruett, a partner at Ernst & Young who advised Allen-Edmonds on production techniques.

Like owners of other small, old-line manufacturing firms, Mr. Stollenwerk also had difficulty persuading some of his 325 production workers to accept change. At the outset, Mr. Stollenwerk thought just-in-time concepts could stem his firm's loss of business from retailers unwilling to wait as many as eight weeks for their shoe orders. He sought to slice overall production time by as much as 87% to five days.

His managers grew confident after their initial success with automating the company's main plant in Port Washington. That factory's floor—where shoe soles and uppers are stitched together and finished pairs boxed for shipping — used to be crammed with unfinished shoes, between work stations. In 1988, the company virtually eliminated the carts by investing $180,000 in a conveyer that transfers work automatically between stations.

Cut Inventory

The move cut the facility's production inventory of unfinished shoes to 1,200 pairs from 5,000, freeing up nearly $400,000 in capital, company officials say. And production time for a pair of shoes dropped to eight hours from 3½ days. People at the plant "were thrilled. The morale was pretty high," says John Gantner, the company's operations manager.

But it wasn't so easy to get suppliers to go along with just-in-time strategy of matching delivery to need. Suppliers of leather soles did agree to make deliveries weekly, rather than monthly, to Allen-Edmonds.

Worst Defeat

But European tanneries supplying calfskin hides refused to cooperate. They stuck with their practice of processing huge quantities of hides at once and wouldn't handle small batches to meet the weekly needs of a small customer, Mr. Stollenwerk says. A bigger customer would have wielded much more power, of course. As a result, Allen-Edmonds still has more than $1 million tied up in monthly inventories of hides.

The just-in-time campaign sustained its worst defeat, however, at the company's Lake Church plant, six miles from the main factory. In a 32,000-square-foot building smelling of hides and leather finishers, workers cut pieces from hides, then sewed them together to make uppers. Seamstresses, paid by piecework, labor intensely. To keep up her pace, one half-seated woman even hurts her body back

Profit Rebound

Sales and pretax profits (loss) for Allen-Edmonds Shoe Corp., in millions

Pretax profits (left scale) -O- Sales (right scale)

1989 1990 1991 1992

Source: Allen-Edmonds Shoe Corp.

and forth between her work pile and her machine.

In 1990, managers rearranged this factory's floor in hopes of reducing the number of unfinished shoes. Figuring that such items spent too much time on the two conveyers, the officials removed one conveyer. The production inventory of uncompleted shoes fell dramatically.

But efficiency *dropped*. Mr. Stollenwerk puts much of the blame on his decision to substitute hourly wages for the company's piecework pay system — a change he considered integral to his just-in-time strategy. "We wanted to see if we could create a new culture," he explains.

Just-in-time theory encourages production workers to focus on quality and teamwork, experts say. Piecework, on the other hand, centers workers' attention on handling individual jobs as fast as possible. Going off piecework "might work great in Japan and southern Illinois, but it didn't work great here. [Our] people needed the discipline that the piecework system gives to them," Mr. Stollenwerk explains.

As productivity plummeted, Allen-Edmonds workers complained about co-workers slacking off. Jacqueline Summers, who makes $9 to $10 an hour, stitching wingtips and other pieces, says she observed "more breaks, more laughing, more giggling." A stitcher must pay attention, she insists, because "you see the same shoe all day long in a nine-hour day, and your eyes can eventually cross."

Reinstated Piecework

Finally, after the company lost $1 million in 1990, it reinstated piecework at Lake Church. Mr. Stollenwerk's managers put more unfinished items back on the factory floor so workers would have more to do. And the executive compromised on his original goal of cutting the company's total production time to five days, settling for two to three weeks instead.

Mr. Stollenwerk says productivity shot back up and in 1991, the company became profitable again. The just-in-time program did save Allen-Edmonds $3.5 million in inventory overhead. The modest improvement in his production time also has helped to retain retailing customers, he adds.

But he grumbles that efficiency experts have yet to come up with a just-in-time solution for small manufacturers, which often require more limited production runs than their bigger rivals.

Some Allen-Edmonds workers long for such a solution, too, because they liked the hourly wage system. Luella Ansay, a 55-year-old stitcher, says that a nine-hour shift of piecework is hard. "Five years ago, I could push it out like you wouldn't believe. But the years go on and you just can't."

PHOTO 14.1

training. When I read the article, I saw right away that the employees wanted nothing to do with the system that was imposed on them. It's very different in our case. Our employees' participation in our decisions shows that we respect them. Because we've won their trust, I'm sure we'll succeed." I let out a great sigh of relief.

That's what unconditional support from senior management looks like!

ATTITUDE OF HONESTY AND OPENNESS TOWARD THE WORKERS

As Gordon put it so well, employee participation in decisions is crucial for succeeding with a large-scale implementation like JIT. By keeping them well informed about our intentions and by sharing our objectives with them, we can count on their cooperation. To get there, we insist on honesty and transparency.

Starting with our very first meeting, where I laid out the problems in our industry and within our company, I was frank and direct with the employees. I had no interest in exaggerating or in manipulating information. The numbers spoke for themselves. Our competitors' bankruptcies were publicly known. Further, the city of Contrecoeur, which had been the Canadian shoe capital just over 50 years earlier, had seen at least four shoe factory closings. I didn't need to draw a picture for the employees. My message was clear: "We can't continue to function this way. We are no longer productive or competitive." I held on to this same integrity throughout the implementation process. For instance, when asked if we could reverse the process in the future, I answered honestly and without beating around the bush: "No!"

FULL COMMITMENT FROM ALL EMPLOYEES

Never before had such direct communication been established with the employees. The company's management had never shared its concerns or objectives with the employees. The employees put forth their maximum effort but they each worked alone. This is why, at our second meeting, when we told them about our intentions to apply the JIT system to the whole factory and asked for their buy-in, many of them were worried. We nevertheless knew very well that the only way to dissipate their doubts and the fears associated with any kind of change was to have them actively participate. We started from the principle that nobody likes to have their behavior dictated without being able to say anything about it; we've all hated that since childhood. And honestly, when we're constrained to silence, how many of us feel motivated, enthusiastic, and happy? By making our employees active stakeholders in the change, we ensured that they would accept the new production method and engage alongside us with confidence.

To encourage participation, we created a committee—named POP, for Production Optimization Project—made up of representatives from the various departments associated with the pilot module's production. The committee chose the types of machine pedals, the height of the tables, the antifatigue mats, the placement of machines and raw materials, the lighting, the plugs, and so forth. They even picked the color we painted the factory walls. They compiled all the information that the engineer received from our manufacturing materials suppliers; no detail was hidden from the group. Every workday ended with a committee meeting to summarize progress and set out the improvements left to make.

The committee's employees later became the project's standard-bearers. Even if the women recognized that they had a hard time at first and that they suffered in the first weeks when they started to work standing up, they nevertheless refused to backtrack.

One thing to never do when you're making a system, process, or machine change is touch the employees' wallets. It's an unwritten law, but nevertheless a clear one. For this reason, when it came time to make promises, I guaranteed to all the employees, on behalf of my employer, that they wouldn't see their salaries drop during or after the transition. This helped me obtain, in return, a guarantee of their participation and their total commitment. Aren't we all more inclined to try something new if we know we're taking no personal risk?

CHOOSING HAND-TO-HAND OR PULL PRODUCTION: SIMPLY INEVITABLE

I cannot insist enough on the importance of hand-to-hand in a pull production* system when it comes to successful JIT implementation. In brief, here are the prerequisites for this kind of production system to work according to forecasts:

- The module *must* be set up in a U-shape.
- The machines *must* be placed in the order of operations.
- The flow in a module *must* work to a *takt** rhythm, at the pace of the pull production.
- Each module's employees *must* be versatile (see Photo 14.2).

Another element of crucial importance: before converting your factory to JIT, make sure that your production materials are ready and that total productive maintenance (TPM)* is correctly implemented. Otherwise, the project could veer toward disaster for your company. Because there is no buffer stock in a JIT system, you need to make sure you've put effective preventive maintenance in place for the machines to avoid breakdowns.

A last piece of advice for successful hand-to-hand: don't slack on employee training. The more you invest at the beginning, the faster you'll get results.

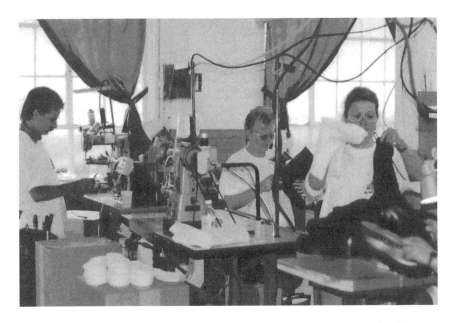

PHOTO 14.2 Versatile employees putting hand-to-hand into practice, one pair of boots at a time.

ASPIRATION TO BECOME A WORLD-CLASS COMPANY

How many times have we heard that this or that manufacturing company is "world class"? But are they really? In my experience, the expression is often misused because it lacks solid criteria. Before my trip to Japan, I had the opportunity to tour a number of factories belonging to so-called world-class high-tech companies in the aerospace and automobile sectors. While many of them publicly posted their objectives of zero accidents, zero defects, and zero stoppages, none were close to reaching them. Unfortunately, none of them would qualify according to the criteria set out below. In my opinion, for a company to be world class, it must

1. Practice JIT within a pull production model.
2. Deliver orders on time in the order they were received.
3. Demonstrate sustained efforts to eliminate all types of *muda**.
4. Integrate templates into its processes to ensure product quality.
5. Maintain a rejection rate below 20 ppm (parts per million).
6. Spare customers the need to inspect your products.
7. Have stock turn over more than 120 times a year.
8. Have an OEE* (Overall Equipment Effectiveness) ratio of over 85%.
9. Work closely with your suppliers and your customers to improve logistics and information processing.

I sincerely believe that we can count on one hand the number of North American factories that would qualify. But the situation may change as the Lean philosophy is implemented in the manufacturing sector.

Genfoot hopes to be one of these world-class companies. In the meantime, we still have a ways to go! And even if we succeed, we'll have to remain vigilant because even once you acquire the status, it must be maintained perpetually.

What about your company? If it meets all the requirements set out above, it's truly world class. Congratulations! For the rest of you, don't give up. If you work hard to apply these standards, you'll likely get there.

Chapter 15

Toyota's Lean Production System, *Kaizen*, and Related Concepts

After World War II, the Japanese economy was in a slump. The manufacturing industry, in particular, was lagging far behind that of the United States. We know that, for instance, before the war, Japanese workers were three times less productive than their German counterparts, and that German workers were three times less productive than American ones. That means that to compete with American workers, the Japanese had to become nine times more productive than they'd been so far. This is the observation that led to the birth of the Toyota Production System* (TPS) as it is known and practiced today.

The origins of *Kaizen** in Japan date back to the postwar period, when American consultants, when helping to rebuild local manufacturing industry, introduced the concept of statistical process control into Japanese factories. Since then, the Japanese have become the masters of its development and application.

TOYOTA PRODUCTION SYSTEM

In August 1945 (the year when Japan lost the war), the president of Toyota, Kiichiro Toyoda, decided to give his company three years to catch up to the manufacturing industry in the United States in terms of productivity. Having become familiar with the Ford production system in the 1930s, he took inspiration from that to develop a Toyota-specific approach. Over the years that followed, he and an engineer named Taiichi Ohno—known for being the designer of the Toyota system—thought about and experimented with different ways of working. Ohno immediately understood that Japanese companies were wasting enormous amounts of money because of rejects and other non-value-added activities. He realized that if he succeeded in eliminating waste, or *muda**, the possibilities were endless. But his main inspiration came from American supermarkets. In self-serve stores (a rarity in Japan at the time),

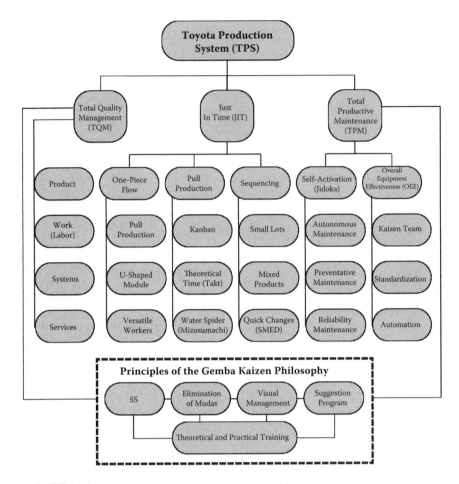

FIGURE 15.1 The Toyota Production System (TPS) and its components.

customers took the products they wanted off the shelves in exactly the quantities that they wanted them, and the shelves were restocked by clerks as needed. Starting with this observation, Ohno developed the concept of pull production*.

Many books have been written about the TPS. Here, an overview of the key ideas will suffice; Figure 15.1 provides a summary. This management method consists of implementing several activities that are so interdependent they can't be pulled apart. They are, among others,

- Process convergence layout
- Implementation of group technology and U-shaped assembly lines
- Adaptation of production lines to be able to vary the models being built
- Development of a versatile workforce that's responsible for product quality
- Preventative maintenance and the rigorous maintenance of production equipment
- Reduced size of production lots

- Elimination of buffer stock
- Just-in-time supplying, meaning in reduced quantities but at more frequent intervals, in a pull production system
- Reduction in machine die-change time
- Participation of all workers in continued improvement projects

The main goal of the TPS is to make it possible to produce several models in small quantities in order to better meet customer needs, with the elimination of *muda* as a starting point. Its three pillars are

- Total quality management* (TQM)
- Just-in-time* production (JIT)
- Total productive maintenance* (TPM), also called production "self-activation," using *jidoka**

Total Quality Management

Paradoxically, while total quality management (TQM) originated in North America in the early 1940s, it's best known through Japan, where it was introduced just after World War II. The "quality" focus that took over in Japan at the time is attributed to two American pioneers, William Edwards Deming and Joseph Juran. Often called "total quality control" (TQC) or simply "total quality," TQM is defined as the application of quality assurance techniques to all of a company's procedures and processes. TQM is based on the idea of quality and respect for customer requirements through the preventive control of processes and services. The tool is part of a continued improvement process where teamwork and worker participation are key, regardless of the workers' hierarchical placement. TQM works through the improvement and measurement of internal procedures, judged more relevant than the financial results obtained using traditional performance ratio calculation. It also includes the quality of systems, work, and services as well as that of the product. The techniques employed to reach total quality are sometimes simple, and sometimes complex. For instance, it can mean a register of production errors that are then discussed in small groups, a re-engineering process, or even research and development workgroups. These days, the application of TQM is almost a guarantee of a company's survival.

At Genfoot, TQM translates into a few basic rules we set for ourselves:

1. Train all workers.
2. Make each defect or problem visible.
3. Make production workers responsible for quality.
4. Make each production worker responsible for his/her own machine maintenance.
5. Ensure that all the products we manufacture go through a defect detection process—no matter what.

We, of course, can't forget the importance of the QCD feedback loop*, meaning the relationship between quality (Q), cost (C), and delivery (D). These concepts are explained in more detail in the next section.

Just in Time, Pull Production*, One-Piece Flow*, and *Takt** Time

To simplify things, we can sum up JIT like this: produce products of superior quality only when ordered, only in the desired quantity, at the best possible cost, and deliver them just in time. To get to this result, you have to eliminate all *mudas* related to the production process.

In keeping with the just-in-time principle, each workstation "pulls"—or takes—the parts it needs to manufacture a product from the workstation preceding it in the sequence of operations. That's what's called "one-piece flow production." The movement from one operation to the next literally happens from hand-to-hand, one item at a time. This production approach prevents any accumulation of materials, or stocking *muda,* between operations.

The shortness of the manufacturing cycle and its efficiency mean that production only starts once a customer order is received. The high flexibility of this approach makes it possible to meet customer needs more quickly and at a lower cost than if the materials and finished products were stocked. To synchronize production and customer demand, we use *takt* time, a theoretical measurement of the expected relationship between the production time of an order and the quantity ordered.

Total Productive Maintenance,
Overall Equipment Effectiveness, and *Jidoka*

The goal of TPM is to optimize the work of equipment by eliminating unplanned stops both small and significant, as well as the kind of "fireman" activities we're used to in the West. It works by using "autonomous maintenance," an expression introduced by the Japan Institute of Plant Maintenance to clearly identify the transfer of responsibility for equipment maintenance to the operator.

One of the most important tools for carrying out TPM is *jidoka**. Widespread in Japan, it's one of the pillars of TPS. It means that a worker or a machine can stop production as soon as an anomaly arises, in order to prevent equipment breaks and the production of defective parts. The devices that make this possible are called *poka-yoke*[†]. These systems make equipment more "autonomous," entrusting them with a relative level of intelligence. As soon

---

* The word *"jidoka"* is translated differently, depending on the source you consult. The term "autonomation" is often used, and also "self-activation." Personally, I prefer to use the Japanese term.
[†] The term *"poka-yoke"* is also used to describe devices that aim to prevent human error.

as they produce lesser-quality parts, overheat, or run out of oil, the machines shut down automatically by activating an *andon**; this signal alerts the worker in charge of maintenance, who can immediately remedy the situation. The implementation of *jidoka* in a company helps reduce the number of operators; a single worker can operate several machines simultaneously, whereas before, four or five workers were needed for the same job. Each operator's productivity is boosted considerably.

Just like TQM, discussed earlier in this chapter, TPM concerns all the company's workers and motivates them to properly maintain their machines. It requires solid basic training. This prepares the operator to carry out a range of tasks, such as daily cleaning and preventive maintenance (including checking lubricant levels and carrying out general inspections) to ensure that the machines work properly. It even prepares them to carry out die or mold changes. This is "autonomous maintenance."

In this context, mechanics are trained to provide technical support to operators, make major repairs, and identify mechanical design problems. As for engineers, they are trained to design equipment that requires minimal maintenance.

Reaching this state is a major step toward being a world-class factory.

TPM goals are as much qualitative as they are quantitative. The most significant qualitative ones include

- Adapting machines to a JIT environment
- A preventative maintenance program applied meticulously
- Training operators to make minor repairs to their own machines
- Improved machine availability
- Collective improvement of the company's culture and image
- Increased skill levels for all workers
- Improvement of the company's overall performance

Quantitative objectives include

- Reduced maintenance costs
- Reduced manufacturing costs
- Reduced reject rate
- Increased revenues generated by improvement to overall equipment effectiveness* (OEE)
- Reduced number of work accidents

In addition to autonomous maintenance, TPM includes other forms of maintenance, such as

- Preventative maintenance: planned stops to inspect and calibrate machines
- Reliability maintenance: priority-setting to reduce the length of repair time and the frequency of outages, the latter dictated by Pareto analyses

All these activities can be summed up by an indicator called "overall equipment effectiveness" (OEE), which measures the efficiency or performance of production equipment and the overall productivity of a production unit. The ratio is a measurement to which Japanese companies attach very high significance. They believe that for their facility to qualify as a world-class factory, it must reach an OEE of 85%.

The OEE is the only indicator that includes all the parameters influencing performance. It's obtained by multiplying Performance by Availability by Quality. So these need to be calculated first in order to obtain the OEE.

The performance rate is given by

$$\text{Performance} = \frac{\text{Ideal cycle} \times \text{output}}{\text{Loading time}} \times 100 \qquad (15.1)$$

where time wastes are related to too-long start-up times and substandard production pace.

The availability rate is given by

$$\text{Availability} = \frac{\text{Operation time} - \text{down time}}{\text{Operation time}} \times 100 \qquad (15.2)$$

where time wastes are caused by outages, die changes, and unauthorized stoppages.

The quality rate is defined as

$$\text{Quality} = \frac{\text{Gross production} - \text{defective products}}{\text{Gross production}} \times 100 \qquad (15.3)$$

where losses are related to defects and rejects due to machines and human error.

Finally, a machine's overall equipment effectiveness can be noted as

$$\text{OEE} = \text{Availability} \times \text{Performance} \times \text{Quality} \qquad (15.4)$$

KAIZEN

The term *"Kaizen"* is made by combining two Japanese words: "kai," which means "change," and "zen," which means "good." The juxtaposition of the two words means "change for the better." The idea comes from the well-known principle of continued improvement. The concept of *Kaizen* was introduced in postwar Japan by American experts who were charged with helping rebuild the country's economy. However, the term and the concept were widely popularized by the book *Kaizen: The Key to Japan's Competitive Success*, published in 1986 by Masaaki Imai, founder of the Kaizen Institute of Japan. He summarized very well the principles of the philosophy by placing them inside a cube that brings together all the elements of *"Kaizen* culture" (Figure 15.2).

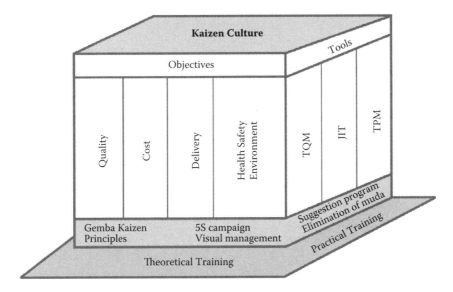

FIGURE 15.2 Various aspects of *Kaizen* culture.

The goal of *Kaizen* is to mobilize all of a company's workers by putting to use their knowledge and talents in order to solve problems and suggest procedure improvements. *Kaizen* is more than just a management style; it's a lifestyle, a state of mind that must be cultivated to inspire workers to invest and innovate. You must think and act *Kaizen*. It's not a system that you can just parachute into an organization. Before even thinking about applying it, you need to set clear objectives and make sure that all the employees understand them. The strategy for getting there combines PDCA* (plan, do, check, act) cycles and SDCA* (standardize, do, check, act) cycles, which maintain the endless loop of continued improvement, along with the application of the tools we discuss at the end of this section.

Kaizen encourages continued improvement in all our activities, but as we can't tackle everything all at once, it's crucial to target the activities that need it the most.

The ultimate goal of *Kaizen* is to produce quality at the best price and in the shortest time possible: QCD*. The three elements of QCD must be mastered in the competitive, fast-changing environment we work in.

As part of the QCD concept, the word "quality" includes not only products and services, but also all the processes related to providing them. The word "cost" represents all the costs engendered from design through manufacturing and sale of a product or service, including after-sales service. Finally, the word "delivery" applies to the manufacturing or the delivery of the product or service. If you improve and optimize these three activities, customers will be satisfied and productivity will climb.

Quality—or lack of quality—plays a determining role in the quest for QCD. Mastering it is indispensable for all manufacturers. When we're fighting for our factory's survival and we compare our manufacturing costs to that of imported products, we can quickly see that eliminating nonquality makes for major savings. The costs of nonconformity, calculated daily in our factories, are an indicator of waste—of raw materials, of machine time, and of labor. A reject must be fixed or thrown out. Repair and replacement create extra expense when it comes to materials and labor. It's easy to understand the influence of quality on cost and production time, but it's also important not to overshoot the customer's quality expectations or needs, aiming for overquality. That will only end up costing more than the customers are willing to pay. In other words, quality doesn't mean perfection; the chosen level of quality must be justified and reasonable.

Kaizen's success in a *gemba* rests on the following pillars:

1. 5S*
2. Standardization
3. Elimination of *mudas*
4. Visual management
5. A suggestion program

These five basic elements are examined in more detail in the following subsections.

The 5S

In his book *Gemba Kaizen: A Commonsense, Low-Cost Approach to Management* (1997), Masaaki Imai sets out a systematic problem-solving approach that starts with the practice of 5S.

The 5S represent five Japanese words: *seiri, seiton, seiso, seiketsu,* and *shitsuke*, which translate as sort, streamline, shine, standardize, and sustain. They can be summed up in one word: cleanliness. The 5S are an indicator of what keeps us from being a world-class factory. A factory where machines and workstations are poorly maintained or where tools are left lying about on tables will definitely end up having human relations problems and low worker participation, as well as producing piles of rejects.

Here's a definition of each of the 5S:

1. *Seiri* (sort) means telling the difference between what's useful or indispensable and what's useless or superfluous, and getting rid of what's not needed. You must absolutely declutter the workstations, removing everything that's unnecessary.
2. *Seiton* (streamline, or set in order) means you need to put away or organize objects in a functional and efficient way. Each object must have a specific place that's clearly identified so that it can be found easily when it's needed.

3. *Seiso* (take care of, or more literally, shine) means cleaning and maintaining work material and the work environment. In addition to reducing accident risk, the fact of having a clean, well-organized work environment has a considerable effect on worker morale and on the quality of work.
4. *Seiketsu* (standardize) means that order, cleaning, and work tool checking must be integrated into the daily routine to keep the work environment in good shape at all times.
5. *Shitsuke* (sustain) means you need to apply the four preceding rules daily and rigorously, so that they become a way of life and part of an endless improvement process.

By adopting and practicing the 5S as a first step in our environment, we set the stage for healthy *Kaizen* management. The 5S create a safe, clean, and pleasant work environment, and help improve the quality of life at work. In this kind of environment, you can expect greater worker motivation and more enthusiastic participation. On the flip side, failure to respect the 5S inevitably produces *mudas*.

*****

The following example (see Photo 15.1) illustrates the effects of applying the 5S method to the organization of the maintenance department at Genfoot. The result is beyond words; see Photos 15.2 and 15.3.

PHOTO 15.1 Work area for the maintenance department before 5S.

PHOTOS 15.2 and 15.3 Same work space with the practice of 5S.

Standardization

By definition, a standard represents the simplest, most effective, and safest way to accomplish a task. But from a *Kaizen* point of view, today's standard is not the best way to do things; it's necessarily improvable.

Establishing a standard may require many years of research, experimentation, and testing. When one is instated, it's accompanied by a procedure that describes the best sequence of operations. By following the procedure, you minimize the variability of results and do away with trial and error. In many cases, standardization means, quite simply, the translation of technical specifications into simple words that an operator can interpret and understand. Once defined, the standard serves to measure an activity, an operation. By comparing a worker's performance to the established standard, you can assess their performance. The standard can also serve to identify the cause of some problems; by analyzing departures from the standard, you can sometimes uncover the source. As needed, the standard is reviewed.

On a broader scale, aren't organizational objectives all based on standards? Don't our quality assurance systems rely on standards and procedures? It's extremely important to identify, define, and standardize all of a company's major activities. This task falls to the administrator. When a reject problem shows up in the *gemba**, the administrator must find the source, take corrective measures, and change the procedures to eliminate the issue. By doing this, they accomplish an SDCA cycle, which consists of standardizing, doing, checking, and acting. The administrator who changes and standardizes a procedure paves the way for the PDCA cycle—plan, do, check, act—where planning takes the place of standardization; the cycle aims to raise the bar on the standard as part of a continued improvement process.

In a *Kaizen* approach, the standard isn't static. It must be revised when a problem occurs. Standardizing the procedure after each problem is an integral part of the QCD optimization process.

Elimination of *Mudas*

In every company, there are daily activities that create absolutely no added value, but that require time or energy and that generate costs. The *Kaizen* philosophy calls these *mudas*, or "wastes." They can be grouped into seven categories:

1. Overproduction *mudas*: These are created when you produce more items than the quantity ordered, whether to avoid the cost of a long start-up (die change) or because you expect a sudden machinery breakdown.
2. Waiting *mudas*: This includes all waiting due to machine malfunctions, tool changes (molds and dies, for instance), or bottlenecks caused by poor layout or poor operation planning.
3. Transportation *mudas*: This includes all handling activities, using manual or electrical dollies, for example, and to the movement of work in process by conveyors during which no value is added to the products (see Photo 15.4).
4. Manufacturing *mudas*: This includes all routine operations carried out on a component that's already machined or molded to compensate for a deficient operation. This is the case, for instance, with the deburring of parts.
5. Stock *mudas*: This includes all stocks of parts that are waiting between various operations, as they are being moved, or resulting from overproduction or "just-in-case" production. These stocks encumber factories that don't practice hand-to-hand.
6. Useless movement and moving-around *mudas*: This includes unnecessary comings and goings, useless movements due to ergonomics problems, and long walks between machines due to layout problems. At Genfoot, one such *muda* occurs when the seamstress takes a piece of fabric from a bin to her left, places it in front of her machine, and sews it for three

PHOTO 15.4 Example of transportation *muda*.

PHOTO 15.5 Example of reject *muda*.

seconds before placing it in a bin to her right. (The total cycle takes ten
seconds, but the value is added only for three seconds.)

7. Defect and reject *mudas*: This includes all rejects caused by poor product design, faulty material, obsolete equipment that continues to generate defective parts, or human error (see Photo 15.5). Often, these
rejects must be repaired or, worse, thrown out. This wastes human and
physical resources.

Kaizen puts forth the simple but effective principle that says we should
keep all activities that add value to the product and eliminate the rest; module
layout, pull production, *jidoka*, total quality, and worker training are the solutions of choice for getting there. But the work doesn't stop there. The *Kaizen*
philosophy means that all efforts are encouraged and deployed to track down
and eliminate each *muda* seen in the company, because eliminating this waste
helps reduce production costs while maintaining product quality, and, in so
doing, significantly improves the company's QCD ratio.

Company managers can use various management tools to eliminate
mudas in their *gemba*. *Gemba Kaizen* focuses particularly on visual management and the suggestion program.

Visual Management

As its name indicates, visual management is management using what you see.
This simple method aims to make visible the problems of all the company's
employees in order to provoke the immediate implementation of corrective
measures. Visual management is a valuable ally of the 5S method. In walking through the *gemba*, you can easily see all the anomalies, whether they're
in the factory's cleanliness, material and equipment defects, or employee
lacunae. For example, just by looking at a machine that produces loads of

rejects, you know it should be equipped with a *jidoka*. As well, just by watching how workers work, you can easily determine whether they master the task or not, and whether they need complementary training. Another example: the stoppage of a machine or assembly chain is a clear sign of a problem. There's nothing more expressive than an inactive production chain and inactive workers! Allowing operators to interrupt production in case of anomaly is therefore visual management.

Visual management in the *gemba* applies to each of the 5Ms*, meaning man, machine, medium, methods, and measurements. Here are a few examples of visible methods and tools for each category:

- *Man (manpower):* Table of skills and absenteeism report posted. Spec sheet installed at each workstation
- *Machine:* Preventative maintenance sheet, *jidoka*, safety devices painted yellow
- *Material: Kanban* in full view on each container of materials, sound or light system that signals a potential shortage of raw material
- *Methods:* Job sequence sheet, machine cycle, target standard, and quality specifications visible at the workstation
- *Measurements:* Color codes identifying operating areas and pressure gauges, graphs of quantities produced and rejects, various goal tables, production calendars, productivity ratios

*****

In all the factories I toured in Japan, the significance placed on visual management was clearly evident. All the *gemba* walls were plastered with graphs and numbers as well as the company's objectives, mission, and customer names. Of course, the numbers and graphs on their own aren't motivational, but when they're seen in relation to objectives, they become so. If you put all these elements in clear view, the workers can make the connection between their own performance and the achievement of the employer's objectives. As a result, they can't help but be more motivated and feel fully invested in the company's success.

Suggestion Program

In every organization, the administrators' challenge is to develop the workers' full potential and profit from it. Managers seek effective ways to motivate and encourage their workers to boost productivity.

It's been proven that even if task standardization is efficient, it's not very motivational. Workers don't like to be treated like robots and perform the same tasks or operations day after day, hour after hour, without having any input into them. To feel motivated, they need to know what's expected of them and feel like their personal involvement makes a difference.

A suggestion program fits perfectly into a *Kaizen* continued improvement philosophy, and it lets employees showcase their skills and creativity. They're even more motivated when they realize that their "volunteer" participation is indispensable to management and is a vital element of the company's success. The suggestion program aims to

- Encourage all workers to take part in improving productivity and the work environment by putting their knowledge to work.
- Reduce or eliminate all *mudas*.
- Promote self-esteem and a sense of belonging with the company.
- Reward initiatives.

But for worker motivation to be maintained, it's essential that the senior management's commitment be constant. Otherwise, the program will run out of steam, and lack of interest will show up quickly. Strong implementation improves communication, encourages camaraderie, and boosts the company's overall productivity.

While one goal of this kind of program is to reduce operating costs, it's clear that savings represent only a tiny portion of the benefits a company can enjoy in regard to all its activities. I personally consider that the most important factor in the suggestion program is that it gives us a way to help each worker consider themselves a full member of the organization and to see that their work, their devotion, and their ideas are directly related to collective success.

The world-class Japanese factories I toured all had suggestion programs in place, and all of the factories stated they got many benefits from them, including

- Increased company profitability
- Improved worker skill
- Improved work methods
- Elimination of all sorts of *mudas*
- Showcasing of work environment problems with a view to their correction
- Better worker motivation
- Better communication and improved interpersonal relations
- A more stimulating work environment
- Stronger ties between management and workers

As for the way to recognize workers' contributions to the suggestion program, theories diverge. Some companies use financial resources because, for them, only money is a motivational factor, while others totally oppose this idea and prefer symbolic gifts. As for me, I think that if money is the only source of motivation, then there's a problem with the company culture. The sense of belonging and the company's success should be most important.

*****

When I toured the Japanese factories, I made a point of examining the practices that were in place for rewarding workers who took part in the suggestion program. I asked every factory manager I spoke with about this. Every time, I got the same answer, more or less. This is the one I got from a manager in the NGK Insulator company:

> The worker who actively takes part in the suggestion program isn't doing it for money, but for the satisfaction of using their creativity and ideas every day with the sole aim of improving their work environment and the quality of their product. The program is, above all, in place to strengthen the sense of belonging and respect toward workers. This is our way of showing them that they are key members of our family and that all their ideas and suggestions count. Our company benefits from their participation as well as from the profits their ideas generate.

However, until I got the answer I wanted in regard to a possible monetary reward, I insisted on details, numbers, graphs, or something else that was concrete. In the end, I got the following explanation:

> There's a financial reward for applied suggestions, but it's not directly proportional to the savings it generates. The reward scale starts at 500 yen for a savings of 55,000 yen. Above 500,000 yen in savings, the reward tops out at 30,000 yen. (These figures are from 2001.)

It's quite true that Japanese workers get the greatest satisfaction when they see their idea described and displayed in the company's main hall or along the factory's corridors. Their name, photo, and a mock-up illustrating the suggestion are part of the company's décor. The savings generated and the worker's reward are also in full view. Some employees make it a point of honor to submit more than 50 ideas a year.

*****

Toyota introduced its first suggestion program in 1951. In 1981, the year of the program's 30th anniversary, 48,757 workers collectively submitted 463,422 suggestions, or nearly 10 per worker; 94% of them were implemented. By its 40th anniversary in 1991, the company estimated that 20 million ideas had been submitted since the program's creation!

Rules for the Smooth Operation of the *Gemba*

For efficient management of the *gemba*'s activities, supervisors and other management team members must make direct contact with the problems that occur. They'll be better placed to fix the difficulties if they apply the following principles:

- **Go to the *gemba*.** The first measure that a manager or supervisor must take when an incident occurs is to get up and go see what's going on with his/her own eyes. The manager can't fix a problem by sitting in an office and listening to a worker describe it. Managers who know their factories well and understand the machines and procedures are better placed to diagnose a problem in short order and come up with a solution. Unfortunately, many Western managers have the bad habit of keeping their distance from problems and unexpected situations, preferring to manage using daily or weekly reports.

• **Examine the *gembutsu**.** The manager who examines the *gembutsu* can often, at a glance, get a good idea of the problem's source. But to get to the bottom of it, he/she also needs to ask the right questions of the workers who are directly involved. *Gemba Kaizen* recommends asking the question "Why?" five times (the Five Whys*) to find the real source of a problem and fix it.

• The following example, drawn from a real problem that came up in our injection plant, reveals the effectiveness of the "Five Whys" approach. One day, the factory maintenance mechanic came to ask me to approve the purchase of sawdust. Remembering an example presented by Masaaki Imai in his book on *Gemba Kaizen*, I started to ask him my questions.

> Question 1: Why do we need sawdust in a plastics transformation factory?
> Answer: To spread around machine number 3.
> Question 2: Why do you want to spread sawdust around machine number 3?
> Answer: To make the floor less slippery!
> Question 3: Why is the floor slippery?
> Answer: Because oil has been leaking from the machine for two days.
> Question 4: Why is it leaking?
> Answer: Because the hydraulic cylinder that activates the mold's opening is leaky.
> Question 5: Why can't we order one and replace it?
> Answer: Uh... Come to think, I think we keep one in stock. I'll go see.

We can see here how asking the right questions makes it possible to identify the core problem.

• **Identify the source of the problem and take temporary corrective measures immediately.** In many cases, you can take an immediate but temporary measure. The short-term goal is to restart the machine as quickly as possible without altering production quality. This solution, for example, may be to get a machine working in manual mode or to add a second operator to take care of the defective device while a spare part is ordered.

• **Standardize to prevent the problem from recurring.** Often, a problem fixed quickly today reappears a few days or weeks later because we didn't take the time to think about it and find a more permanent solution. In many cases, workers who have already seen a problem solve it automatically, without trying to eliminate the true source. Often, we pick the simplest or fastest solution rather than the right one.

For example, to go back to the example of the machine that's leaking oil and the sawdust, the worker judged that it would be simpler to spread sawdust around the machine to absorb the oil than to take the time to replace the machine's cylinder, even if the second solution would save money and be more effective in the long term. Often, this isn't bad faith or laziness, because they may well think that they're helping out the employer and saving them money.

But why allow a problem to recur? Isn't there a prevention procedure? In the *Kaizen* philosophy, every temporary problem fix must be followed by a standardized procedure to end up with a definitive solution. This is everyone's business, but the manager must initiate it.

TOYOTA PRODUCTION SYSTEM AND *KAIZEN* IN BRIEF

The TPS's jargon can be complicated, and some authors' habit of calling the system all sorts of other names doesn't help make anything simpler. So there's often confusion about the meanings of the associated terms. They can seem redundant but, although inseparable, they are distinct. For example, we hear *kanban*, pull production, value-added Lean* production, or even *Kaizen* system instead of Toyota Production System. However, while all these are part of the TPS, they aren't synonymous; they are each tools or methods that Toyota uses to reach its objectives.

To achieve QCD objectives (quality, cost, delivery) and those relative to health, safety, and environment (left side of the cube), we use three tools: total quality management (TQM), just in time (JIT), and total productive maintenance (TPM) (right side of the cube). Each of these has its own field of application. TQM deals with total quality at all levels and in all company activities. JIT relates to all aspects of production, cost, and delivery, while TPM concerns the reliability of production equipment. That said, there's a certain feedback loop between the three tools. TQM and TPM must be implemented and integrated into work habits before you even think about implementing JIT. Imagine a JIT context where you decide to reduce the stock of work in process without having thoroughly seen to the preventive maintenance of your machines. They'd each end up having outages, one after the next, and that would cause stock shortages and delivery delays.

Never forget that for it to succeed, the *Kaizen* philosophy must be implemented everywhere, at every level of the company: production workers, first-line supervisors, managers, and factory manager. The company's upper management must cultivate and encourage it by creating a favorable work environment, a climate where each worker feels like a full member of a big family and doesn't hesitate for a second to put forth their ideas for improvements.

The objectives and methods for achieving this all rest on the same foundations: solid theoretical and practical training for all the organization's workers, as well as the rigorous application of basic *gemba* management rules, elimination of *mudas*, 5S campaigns, standardization, and visual management.

All these activities, practiced simultaneously, lead to *Kaizen* culture, which is the ultimate goal, and from there, the achievement of QCD.

Chapter 16

Tour of World-Class
Japanese Factories

In June 2001, I have the pleasure of touring world-class Japanese factories in Nagoya and Toyota City*. This is part of the *Gemba Kaizen*™ and JIT (just-in-time) training given by the Kaizen Institute of Japan. I get to see the following factories up close:

- Toyoda Iron Works
- Yamaha Motors
- NGK Insulators (Chita factory)
- Togo Seisakusho
- Taiho Kogyo
- Toyota (Takaoka factory)

What these factories have in common is that they practice JIT*, TPM*, and TQM*. Of course, those are prerequisites for becoming a world-class factory!

Before setting off to learn about Japanese know-how, we have a first group meeting led by Mr. Masaaki Imai, the guru of *Kaizen* and *Gemba Kaizen* in Japan. He asks us to introduce ourselves and to state our expectations and objectives for the training we're about to take. In hearing the names on the participant list, I notice that I'm the only North American signed up. A number of Europeans and Asians are present; they work in the automobile industry and elsewhere. For a short moment, I fear that the training will be given in Japanese because I forgot to check this detail when I registered. Fortunately, that's not the case! I'm even surprised to note that Mr. Imai speaks perfect English.

---

* Note that the information provided in this chapter on the companies I visited, such as sales figures and certifications, reflects what was true at the time of my tours.

When my turn comes, I introduce myself as follows:

"Hi, my name is Joe Bichai. I'm the vice-president of manufacturing with the Genfoot company in Canada. We're the country's leading outdoor boot manufacturer and we operate four factories in North America. About eight years ago, we converted our biggest factory to TPS and modular manufacturing. I think we've reached 90% of our productivity objectives but I feel like we're starting to stagnate. I hope to find the solution here that will help us reach our objectives at 100% and become a world-class factory."

After a dream week for an industrial engineer, we come back together as a group for a last meeting. Each participant has to speak about his/her impressions. This time, I make the following declaration:

"When I introduced myself at the beginning of the week, I told you that our objective of having a world-class factory had been 90% reached, and I was hoping to find the solution to get the missing 10%. Today, I'd like to restate my idea. After touring the factories and talking with their managers, I realize that we've actually still got 90% to go in order to become world class. We have accomplished a lot in the last eight years, but there's still an enormous amount of work to do. However, I'm sure we're on the right track. As the managers of all the factories we toured bear witness, what we've seen is the result of several decades of JIT, TPM, and *Kaizen*. Thanks, and good luck to everyone in your projects."

What happened during that week for my perception to change so radically? To explain, I'll share with you the experience of my six tours.

TOYODA IRON WORKS

I tour the main factory of this multinational auto parts manufacturer. Its manufacturing procedures include the drawing, welding, painting, and assembly of components such as handbrakes, gas pedals, brakes, and clutches, as well as suspension and radiator supports.

Established in 1949, the company is certified ISO 9001. It has received many excellence awards, including supplier of the year for Toyota, for both the quality of its products and the excellence of its technology, for five consecutive years.

During the tour, I notice in particular the movements of the *kanbans*, the supply of assembly modules every 10 minutes, and the fact that manufacturing is done in U-shaped modules. I also witness applications of SMED* (Single-Minute Exchange of Dies) when, in less than two minutes, they change the dies in a 1,600-ton press.

From the second I step into the factory, I'm flabbergasted at the level of cleanliness. After all, it's a transformation factory! The entire floor is painted: the alleyways, storage areas, and production floor are in different colors. Everything is visual. There are signboards everywhere! At each workstation, an example part is displayed in full view with all the necessary specifications.

The factory assembles 2,100 different components. Toyota specified in its contract that it requires a reject rate of less than 15 ppm (parts per million). The company set its own objective of 10 ppm. At the time of my tour, the actual reject rate is 2.02 ppm. Incredible!

The company has 1,965 employees, of which 877 perform direct labor and 1,088 indirect labor (meaning labor that does not add value to the product, such as material handlers and mechanics). This indirect/direct ratio is, in my humble opinion, very high for a manufacturing company. At the time of my tour, 28% to 30% of workers are temporary (I explained this point in the section titled Japanese Factories Offer Their Workers Lifelong Employment, Chapter 17). When they're hired, workers get four hours of training before meeting their supervisor. The supervisor takes them to their module, where the new workers take the rest of the day to observe the operation they'll be performing the next day. The workers devote the first 3 minutes of their day to reading the product specifications and the last 5 minutes to cleaning up their workstations in keeping with the 5S principle. Only 40 minutes of in-process goods are allowed at any given time in the production area.

Toyoda moved into JIT and *kanban* in 1972. It wasn't until 1993 that they really took up *Kaizen*. This initiative helped it reduce its delivery time, which dropped from 5.7 days to 3.2 days, from order reception to product delivery.

I make my first stop at the shipping and receiving dock. That's where the whole supply chain starts. A truck is backing into the parking spot set aside for it. It was expected at 2:15 p.m. and it's now 2:18 p.m. Unlike what's done in North America, the truck doesn't come to the dock; it parks in the street. The truck's side panels lift to facilitate the maneuvers. The driver does his own unloading and deposits his cargo at the factory entrance at a precise spot. Squares, each the size of a pallet, are painted straight onto the floor with the number of components that must be left there. To finish up, the driver heads to the planning service, where he places the *kanban* envelopes for each product delivered into their respective slots. Every time he deposits an envelope, a light-sensitive detector lights up a green signal that lets the planner know about a new arrival. The driver also has to pick up the *kanbans* for the empty containers that he needs to bring back to the supplier to start another production cycle. The parts are delivered at 10-minute intervals. If the delivery is more than 15 minutes late, a red signal alerts the planner.

When the driver fills up his truck, the *kanbans* are gathered up and inserted into a sorter similar to a bank's money-counter. The device is linked with a printer, which produces the invoice accompanying the cargo. Very efficient!

In the factory, I can see up close all the JIT and *Kaizen* practices in the *gemba*. I'm right in the heart of the action. For example, I get to watch a versatile worker work in a handbrake assembly module. The woman, in her sixties, is alone, operating 10 automated machines. She assembles a complete brake. Depending on the order, she can make one of nine different models and up to 60 die changes within a single day. The lots vary from one to six parts per box. The plastic box that holds the lots includes a foam insert designed for six parts. The die changes are done using a small dolly, and they take 50 to 90 seconds. The raw materials are delivered every 10 minutes. Everything's within reach: raw materials, boxes, quality gauges, and so forth. If the die that the worker changes isn't perfectly positioned, a red signal lights up and every-thing stops. This is what we call *jidoka* (an automatically activated device), and it makes it possible to do *poka-yoke*, meaning to prevent all manufacturing errors. The assembly cycle for a handbrake is 15 minutes. The *mizusumashi** resupplies the module every 15 minutes as well. The worker never waits in front of her machine for the operation to be fully executed. Once she has activated the machine, she leaves it to do its work and moves on to the next machine, where another part is waiting. There is no waiting *muda*!

In other modules, robots perform the die changes. They're placed on a shelf next to the press. They weigh between 55 and 110 pounds. The change never takes more than 60 seconds. As for giant-sized dies, which measure over 9 by 17 feet and are used on presses weighing over 1,000 tons, their setup time is under two minutes. The change is made using a giant transporter on rails. An operator standing in front of his press yells the entire time the die change is happening. (I wonder what kind of bug bit him, but our guide explains that he's checking the steps of the operation out loud to ensure that he doesn't forget anything.) Once the new die is in place, a supervisor whistles to alert all the module's workers that the press is going to be turned on again. The entire spectacular operation, this time, takes exactly 72 seconds. That's pretty incredible, especially know-ing that this kind of change could take over four hours in another factory!

YAMAHA MOTORS

This multinational, reputed for the quality of its recreational products, manu-factures more than 2 million units per year and employs over 10,000 people. All-terrain vehicles, outboard motors, boats, and motorcycles make up the bulk of their annual sales. Yamaha has 10 factories within a 12-mile radius. The one I tour assembles motorcycle chassis at a pace of 700 units per day. Certified ISO 9003 and ISO 14000 in 1999, the factory practices 5S and visual man-agement techniques everywhere. *Andons** are in place at various steps of the process and indicate the quantities produced and the standards in real-time. The factory is highly automated. More than 80 robots work on the assembly lines, whose pace is dictated by the speed of a conveyor. Yamaha uses a mixed production system, where five or six motorcycle models can be assembled simultaneously. The workstations are supplied by self-guided vehicles.

The company is very proud of the efforts it is deploying in TPM*, and with reason. It decided to implement TPM in all its activities in 1984. Just five years later, in 1989, it received the most sought-after TPM excellence award.

The company launched hundreds of small *Kaizen* improvement projects, which made for considerable savings.

I really like the colored "alert codes" on the shelves and components; when the parts are used up or removed from the shelves, a green- and red-painted area announces the stock outage to the worker.

Upon hiring, a new worker has to intern at the company's training and professional development center. Simulation stations are set up for exercises.

The company launched a remarkable program to turn its 44 supervisors into qualified TPM trainers. They, in turn, have to train the hundreds of workers in their charge. Frequent tests demonstrate the operators' skills in maintenance work for the various machines.

That said, despite its impressive level of automation, its 5S and visual management practices, its TPM, and its suggestion program, I must admit that I'm really disappointed in this factory. I can't consider it a world-class factory because I notice a number of lacunae, including multiple sources of *muda*. For example, I see no U-shaped modules, but instead assembly chains where workers wait for the next motorcycle to show up (waiting *muda*). As well, the workstations aren't well designed or ergonomic. There are no multidisciplinary teams or *kanbans*. And the goal of a 0.5% reject rate (we're far from the 2.02 ppm at the Toyoda factory!) and 85% OEE* are not yet reached. This is proof that it's not easy to reach the status of world-class factory, and that only the sustained application of TQM, JIT, and TPM makes it possible to attain.

NGK INSULATORS, CHITA FACTORY

This Japanese multinational company, with 4,500 employees, produces ceramic insulators for electrical installations. NGK is the world's largest manufacturer of this type of product, and it exports its production all over the world. The factory I toured (in Chita) launched TPM in 1994. It won the TPM Excellence Award in 1998. It is also certified ISO 9001 and ISO 14001.

The benefits of its TPM implementation are impressive, as shown in Table 16.1.

Getting this kind of result in only four years is truly phenomenal. This TPM was made possible thanks to a suggestion program. The program received 43,000 ideas in 2001, against 68,000 two years earlier. When questioned about this drop, our guide explains that the company insisted that year on the quality of suggestions instead of their quantity. The program enjoys a participation rate of 62.3% and an average of 10 suggestions per worker. A single worker submitted 50 ideas this year, meaning an average of one per week! All over the factory, the suggestions are posted along with the name and photo of their authors, who have generated savings to the tune of 134 million yen.

TABLE 16.1 Examples of Benefits Resulting from MPT at NGK Insulators

	Before TPM	After TPM
Productivity	100%	171%
OEE ratio	67%	85%
Lead time	102 days	69 days
Work accidents	100	0

Source: Kaizen Institute of Japan.

Before TPM was introduced, the company was facing fairly serious problems, such as

- Unqualified operators
- Low morale in the factory
- Insufficient product quality
- Drop in market share
- Frequent, unexpected machine stops
- Lack of safety in the workplace

The company decided to train all its workers. It set up a classroom for theory and hands-on classes where workers learned about machine maintenance before returning to work in the factory. That's where they tried their hand, until they mastered the procedures and were able to diagnose and correct all possible problems with the machinery they had to operate. To help them, in the room there were samples of rejects displayed with possible causes identified. Each worker trains 20 days a year, two consecutive days at a time.

Visual management is used to a very high degree at the factory, where operations are, by nature, dirty and loud. Here, it's not limited to signboards and giant graphs. All sorts of control lists are posted everywhere. Lines and arrows are painted on the floor to indicate to operators where the shelf is with the part they're looking for; and all the pressure gauges are equipped with stickers identifying normal zones in green and problem zones in red. This way, the operators can see anomalies at a glance.

The factory contains more than 450 different machines. The raw materials are primarily silica and sand. They're ground up, pulverized, and mixed with clay. The resulting paste is then kneaded, worked, and extruded in the form of immense six-and-a-half-foot-tall cylinders. The cylinders are then baked in a ceramic oven. Finally, they're machined, polished, and cut.

I was expecting that activities like this would produce tons of dust and an infernal racket, and that there would be water all over the floor. Quite the opposite! All the raw material conveyors are confined in transparent plastic tubes, and the hood inputs are protected by rubber flaps. As well, dusters are omnipresent at every step of production.

In short, the training helped workers to master the procedures, solve problems, and respect production standards, while small TPM improvements and self-activated maintenance succeeded in eliminating water, air, and oil leaks, as well as noise and dust.

This world-class factory succeeded in bringing its OEE rate from 67% in 1994 to 85% in 1998. The year of my tour, the objective was 93%!

TOGO SEISAKUSHO

This 100-year-old company manufactures springs, connectors, and electronic components. Togo has nearly 800 employees and produces 1.5 million springs a day! In all, it makes 200,000 deliveries of 20,000 items to 300 different customers per month, 99.97% of which arrive on time! At the time of my tour, it was certified QS-9000, ISO 9001, and ISO 14001, and counted Toyota, Mitsubishi, and Isuzu among its largest customers. The walls of the company's entrance hall are festooned with excellence awards for quality, TPM, design, and more.

Imagine 60 stamping presses, 40 injection machines, and hundreds of small automated machines designed and built by the company itself. They're all equipped with problem detection mechanisms (*jidoka**). Little robots that separate the parts and control tolerances are placed near each machine. Operators are an endangered species in this ghost factory. The presses are all automatic.

The factory is impeccable and its floor is immaculate. There are no oil leaks under the presses. No workers standing immobile in front of machines. A level of automation I'd never have believed possible! All the machines are in process convergence. SMED, TPM, TQM, JIT, it's all there! A real world-class operation. The only *muda* the factory manager points out is the team of 10 employees inspecting miniature springs. The precision they're looking for (0.01 millimeters) is so strict that even vision systems mounted on the presses aren't precise enough. For this company, inspection equals *muda*!

At Togo, the operators are trained to make their own mold and die changes, and to do preventive maintenance on their machines. They only call the mechanic in case of major outage. The mold setter job as we know it in North America doesn't exist. The factory manager can barely believe me when I explain that we have three people who do only this; he doesn't understand why we're paying these people in addition to operators whose machines are stopped. In his company, the planned stop of the machines takes place twice a year: 10 days in May, 10 more in August, and a few days' closure at Christmas. Still, I'm proud to tell him we only have a single mold setter per work shift.

All the factory's workers have at least a high school–level education. This is a key prerequisite because they need to be able to read and interpret very complex and precise technical drawings.

In conclusion, having worked in injection factories and managed them for many years, I'm floored by this factory's cleanliness and efficiency. I'd heard the expression "so clean you could eat off the floors," but to see it in the *gemba* is quite something! I'll never again accept it when my factory managers tell me we have to spread absorbent around leaking machines.

TAIHO KOGYO

Founded in 1944, this 1,200-employee company produces and sells precision parts cast in aluminum for the automobile market. It ships 11 million parts per month. At the beginning of 2000, its sales surpassed 42 billion yen. It was certified ISO 9001 and QS-9000 in 1997. As well, it received several excellence awards, such as Q1 from Ford, QE from Chrysler, TQC from Toyota, and PM and TPM awards. Not surprising, considering we know that it launched TPM activities more than 30 years ago. This tour gets me particularly excited because I can see numerous simple and practical applications of TPM and TQM.

Above all, I'm impressed by the 30 production chains, each made up of 16 different machines, all linked with one another, with *one single* operator to change the dies and handle maintenance. That operator can make up to 20 dies changes per day. I don't need to give you the details of the training program they have in place; I'm sure you can imagine its scope. Let's just note that the operator writes the maintenance and repair manual for his own machine. Amazing! The management regularly evaluates each worker's progress.

As in all world-class factories, the practices of 5S, visual management, TPM, and JIT mark all the company's activities. It functions by pull production, and *kanban* is the only control tool for the process downstream. The best practices of the *gemba* are also in evidence. Pareto* diagrams illustrating *gembutsu** and ideas for improvements by eliminating various *mudas* are posted all over the factory's walls. And what cleanliness for a transformation factory!

During this tour, I have the chance to observe a *Kaizen* team at work. Made up of 10 workers from various departments with a range of skills, it visits problem workstations, observes operations, evaluates the changes to be made, and implements them immediately. This can mean a rearrangement of the workstation, or purchasing or making changes to existing equipment. This "commando" team is part of the problem-solving philosophy that's based on using the company's internal resources and the synergy of skills. It may work four to eight hours at a time as needed.

All over the factory, I see posters with the number "3" in evidence. Because I can't read Japanese, I ask our interpreter what the signs mean. He explains that the general continued improvement objective is to reduce costs by 3%. This reduction rate applies to materials saved, unplanned outages and stoppages avoided, fewer rejects, and so forth. All the results obtained in line with this are exhibited in full view of the workers and updated daily. Even the factory's accounting is done every night!

TOYOTA, TAKAOKA FACTORY

Finally, it's the big day! The one I've been waiting for since I heard about the Toyota system in 1982. We're expected at the Takaoka factory at 9:30 a.m. Our bus arrives at 9:15 a.m., but with a view to decorum, we certainly wouldn't walk in early. The driver decides to give us a little 15-minute tour before pulling up at the reception station at the factory entrance.

---

* The Pareto diagram is a simple method for filing data in size order: it's a block graph with the highest columns on the left and the lowest on the right. A "totals" row indicates the relative height of the columns. This diagram comes from the Pareto principle, also known as the "20/80 rule," because Vilfredo Pareto, economist and sociologist, demonstrated in the early twentieth century that 20% of the population of Italy held 80% of the country's wealth.

At the appointed hour, an interpreter-guide greets us at the door and comes onto the bus to escort us to the factory entrance. During our little 10-minute stroll, we're bombarded with facts and figures, each more impressive than the previous one. Founded in 1937 by Sakichi Toyoda, Toyota today employs more than 65,000 people and posts sales of 7,408 billion yen all over the world. In 2000, it built and sold more than 3.4 million vehicles and never stopped taking over areas of the very competitive automobile market. At the time, their share was around 34%. Unlike its biggest competitors (GM, Ford, and Chrysler), Toyota posted solid profits year after year, like a metronome, recession or no recession! This profit sat at 329 billion yen for the year 2000.

The Takaoka factory opened in 1966; it was Toyota's second one. It covers an area of 5.4 million square feet. It operates on two work shifts and employs 6,000 people to produce 2,800 cars in six different models per day. A car comes off the assembly line every 45 seconds. The manufacturing time from the first stamping operation to the moment a car leaves the factory is 20 hours! Unlikely, you say? True! When you consider that a car is made up of an average of 30,000 parts and that 150 external suppliers deliver 1,500 different parts (which requires quite the supply coordination), it's beyond impressive!

The factory is a real monument to the glory of productivity. None of the books I read could have expressed what I'm seeing. I could write a book just on this tour, it's so mind-boggling. The overall view from the top of the catwalk reminds me of a concert hall, where everything is magnificently orchestrated. I see and appreciate the genius behind this production masterpiece. All the activities follow one another in perfect cadence, each team member knows exactly what to do, and all the parts converge toward the same chain—no hesitations, no errors! The level of automation is very high at every step of production: it's 99% for assembly and 100% for stamping. What a rousing spectacle! You may think I'm getting carried away by my enthusiasm, but let me tell you a bit more about this perfection.

Imagine a final assembly line that produces six different models of cars at the same time, toward which converge a hundred subassembly lines where several hundred workers are on task. The assembly line doesn't stop. Assembly and external suppliers are synchronized to the factory's *takt* time, which is 45 seconds. The engine chain, which also converges toward the final assembly line, includes a hundred operations and subassemblies.

Doors of different models and colors come out of the painting line (it, too, synchronized with the final assembly line), move along an overhead conveyor, and arrive at the operator at the exact second he needs them. Because of the wide variety of colors and models, the assembler can easily install a red door on a Corolla, followed by a black one on an Echo. When he turns to grab the next door, he doesn't hesitate for a single second. He could just as well lift it with his eyes closed and have no fear of making a mistake: it's the right one. Same thing for the motors that end up on the final assembly line. At four, six, or eight cylinders, the right engine always shows up for the right car. This precision applies to all the other components, such as dashboards, seats, windshields, and so forth.

Can you envision the show a little better? A satellite detection system ensures that all these parallel activities work perfectly in sequence. A little antenna is installed at the start of the line on the body; it's only removed at the final operation. The radiofrequency system transmits instructions to the robots on the converging lines and manages the order of parts. The *kanbans* with all the relevant instructions are placed on the products coming out of the painting line. They also serve as preventive measures so that the right part arrives at the right place when it's needed.

The factory is unbelievably clean. The aisles are painted in one color, the halls in another color. The robots and all the machines with moving parts are fenced off. The workers' ergonomics, health and safety, and well-being are respected.

All the concepts that JIT fans study and scrutinize are embedded into the workers' mentality. The practice of 5S, the elimination of *muda*, visual management, TPM, *jidoka*, TQM, JIT, multidisciplinary teams, U-shaped chains, process convergence production, SMED, mixed chains, and suggestion programs are all in evidence throughout the factory. I've been here for barely three hours, and my last year of industrial engineering studies and my 20 years of professional practice are all playing out before my eyes. If we didn't have a tour of the Toyota head office planned, I'd stay much longer to watch and learn! However, we have a lunch awaiting us and a question period, which I'm very much looking forward to. During our tour, I've taken 10 pages of notes and I have a few questions that our guide wasn't able to answer. The other members of the delegation have their own questions, which seem just as interesting.

In summary, here are the results of our discussions with the Toyota representatives:

Question: With a 45-second *takt* cycle, the operator can't hesitate or make a mistake. What happens if he picks up the wrong part?
Answer: When an operator on the production chain turns to pick up parts from a container, he can't make a mistake. He can pick it up with his eyes closed, because the parts are designed to prevent errors. Each part has a specific design and can only be assembled the right way! As well, the smaller parts are kept separately in their containers to make them easier to pick up.
Question: Do non-module workers still rotate?
Answer: On the assembly lines for cars or engines, the workers rotate every two hours.

(The following questions are my own.)

Question: I noticed that your workers don't wear uniforms, unlike those in the other factories we toured. What's the reason for this?
Answer: We had uniforms for years. But through our suggestion program, a worker proposed that we get rid of uniforms and save more than $100,000 a year. So we did it.

Question: Are you satisfied with your suggestion program? Do you find that after a few years, programs like this run out of steam and need reinvigoration?

Answer: We're very satisfied with the program. Last year, we received an average of 35 suggestions per worker, which is pretty spectacular. To keep workers motivated to take part in the program, we posted a thought from our founder all over the factory: "*Kaizen* is in the air. You need to always think *Kaizen*, breathe *Kaizen,* and feel *Kaizen!*"

Question: I noticed that, just before the lunch break, the *andon* for the main line indicated that you were six cars late with 97% efficiency. What happens in this kind of situation?

Answer: If the workers can't make up for this lateness during regular work-hours, they'll have to stay late to finish production.

Question: Are they paid for this catch-up time, or do they need to take responsibility and do it at their own cost?

Answer: When they work after regular hours, they're paid overtime.

(I have a hard time accepting this answer from the factory manager.)

Question: If the worker is getting paid at time and a half, wouldn't he want to slow down the chain in order to earn more money?

(The manager takes a somewhat offended tone.)

Answer: The worker would be ashamed to call home and say he'll be late. He knows he hasn't accomplished what his employer expected of him. He'll go home with his head bowed in shame!

(I think to myself: head bowed, but pockets full! I wonder what his wife would think. But we're allowed to disagree with some Japanese practices!)

Chapter 17

Myths and Realities
of Japanese Industry Workers

Quite a few ideas are floating around about Japanese employees and companies. These four often come up:

1. Japanese people are very disciplined workers with great respect for authority.
2. Japanese companies offer their workers lifelong employment.
3. In the Toyota system, every worker is authorized to halt the assembly chain.
4. In Japan, rejects are measured in parts per million rather than by percentage.

Do these reflect reality? Utopia? A false perception? If we look at them more closely, we can separate myth from fact and bring some nuance to the discussion.

JAPANESE WORKERS ARE VERY DISCIPLINED
AND RESPECT AUTHORITY MUCH MORE
THAN WORKERS IN OTHER COUNTRIES

This couldn't be truer. Perhaps it's a cultural trait. In my extensive travels, I've never encountered a people more disciplined and respectful than the Japanese. In personal contexts, the people I've met are courteous and kind. But in the *gemba**, they change their behavior radically. For them, *gemba* is not a place to socialize, laugh, or chat about subjects other than work. And this is true for both factory workers and bosses. You never see two workers from the same module talking as they watch their automated process work. If a boss addresses them, they stand up straight and listen attentively to instructions, bowing their heads to show they've understood.

When I took a tour of world-class factories, I visited one that manufactured small injection-molded, high-precision connectors. I was fascinated to see some 40 machines operating apparently without any employees at the helm. You see, in Japan it is very rare to see an employee camped out in front of a single machine, and even less so in a world-class business. In the factory in question, each operator is in charge of 10 machines; so they have to move from one machine to the next based on need. Their responsibility includes changing molds, setup, maintenance, and quality control.

During my tour, I attentively observed a machine made up of a robot mounted on an injection machine. It removed the runners from four cavities, optically measured the interior diameter to separate the parts by size, and deposited them into their respective boxes. The rejected runners ended up in a small red box. They went through a shredder to be recycled. The machine's total cycle was 20 seconds. When I saw the robot reject three consecutive parts from the same cavity, I stopped to examine the operation. I figured the rejected parts must not have been needed for the order they were in the process of preparing, and that it would be preferable to block the plastic supply to the cavity than to mold a part and then reject it. In our North American factories, this could have been par for the course and gone unnoticed; but for a company that needs to present a rejection rate below 20 parts per million (ppm), such a situation could cause panic! When the factory director approached me to ask me to follow the group, I showed him the cavity the rejected parts came from, and asked if it wouldn't be better to block it. From his face, I could tell there was a problem. He left us for a few seconds and signaled to the employee responsible for the machine to approach. The director, pointing to the reject box, spoke for a couple of minutes in a brusque but polite tone, a cascade of words. I would have loved to understand what he was saying! The operator, standing ramrod-straight, nodded his head and cried, "Hai!" every four or five words to indicate that he fully understood the message. I felt a bit embarrassed to watch the scene, but happy to have seen with my own eyes a director speaking to a worker in the *gemba*. When I rejoined my group, I told our Japanese interpreter what I'd just seen. I added that the poor operator must have been furious to be spoken to like that in front of visitors. To my great surprise, the interpreter explained that the employee must of course have been angry, but at himself, because he had just disappointed his boss. He had let his employer down, and worse still, in front of visitors. From my point of view, the operator's mistake wasn't really that serious, especially because he had to watch the production of 10 machines; he couldn't be everywhere at once! But that's the mentality in a Japanese *gemba*!

JAPANESE FACTORIES OFFER THEIR WORKERS LIFELONG EMPLOYMENT

A few decades ago, this was true for most major companies. They offered a job to each of their employees until they retired. But this trend is fading.

It must be said that the postwar "Japanese economic miracle" has run out of steam, and the country has had to face a number of financial crises starting in the mid-1980s, including three recessions since 2010[*]. As a result, even in 1995, only 40% of companies were still offering lifetime employment; by the mid-2000s, the number was more like 30%[†].

The lifetime employment system has many merits: it strengthens the employee's loyalty to the employer, makes employees feel secure about their jobs, and allows companies to invest more in training and education because they're practically certain to keep the employees they've trained. But it can also be harmful when it comes to labor costs and company productivity. As employees age, they become a burden on the employer because it's more difficult to adapt to technological change. So they're assigned nonspecialized work. But in this way, their salaries become much higher than the value of their work because, in Japan, assembly workers' salaries are among the highest in the world. For instance, in 2001, when I was touring Japanese factories (see Chapter 16), I was told that a Toyota worker cost his employer 4,000 yen per hour (about CAN$52), including a bonus and benefits worth about 31.5%.

To reduce their costs, Japanese companies now tend to hire up to 30% temporary labor. When production drops or process automation leads to a reduction in jobs, the temporary employees are laid off, while permanent employees are offered jobs on another production chain in the same factory, or as needed in a neighboring factory.

There is another situation that will influence the Japanese job market in the coming decades: the country is facing a serious problem with regard to the aging of its population. In 2010, 23% of the total population were aged 65 or over, and it's estimated that by 2050, this percentage will rise to almost 40%[‡]. This is why Japan has decided to push back the legal retirement age from 60 to 65; the measure will gradually take effect between now and 2025[§].

IN THE TOYOTA SYSTEM, ANY WORKER CAN HALT THE PRODUCTION CHAIN

This is not a myth. In fact, it's a principle that makes perfect sense in a JIT* environment; it is indispensable to reaching *Kaizen** objectives. In Chapter 15 we learn about the importance of *jidoka** for individual machines and the need to stop them instead of producing rejects. The same principle applies to

---

[*] OECD. 2013. Japan towards a new dynamic growth – Highlights from the 2013 OECD Economic Survey of Japan.

[†] Data provided by the Kaizen Institute of Japan during my 2001 training.

[‡] National Institute of Population and Social Security Research in Japan. "Population projections for Japan (January 2012): 2011 to 2060." [Online] www.ipss.go.jp/index-e.asp Wikipedia. 2013. "Aging of Japan." [Online] (accessed February 20, 2014).

[§] Matsuyama, Kanoko. 2012. "In Japan, retirees go on working." www.businessweek.com, August 30, 2012. [Online] www.businessweek.com/articles/2012-08-30/in-japan-retirees-go-on-working. Accessed February 20, 2014.

the production chain. At the first anomaly, even a small one, the employee must stop the chain. This is the only way to prevent the creation of reject or repair *mudas**.

However, when *jidoka* prevents a machine from producing rejects on a production chain by stopping it, by the same token it can paralyze 10 others that are linked in pull production*. And the situation is even rougher on the final production chain in the Toyota factory because its stoppage can have repercussions on the work of several thousand employees. In this company, the entire factory and its suppliers are synchronized to a 45-second *takt** cycle. A worker who stops the chain is very aware of the consequences of his/her action. That said, because the idea of stopping the chain has been taught to them since the moment they were hired, they know that the company encourages them to do so when needed.

During my tour of Toyota's Takaoka assembly factory in Toyota City, our guide explained the way an emergency stop works. According to the guide, it happened very rarely but it could occur at any time. And, in fact, a few minutes later—surprise!—I saw an employee making an emergency stop.

I was standing on a bridge over the production chain, so I was in a perfect position to observe the scene. One of the operations consisted of placing the dashboard and fastening it with four screws. While he was placing a dashboard in a car, the employee noticed that the right side of the part wasn't fitting. He tried to make up for it by inserting the two sides simultaneously. Nothing worked! Without further ado, he pulled the emergency cord. The events that unfolded in the seconds that followed were worthy of a Hollywood script. Once the signal was given, the *andon** showed the problem spot and its place in the chain. Suddenly, the supervisor, emerging out of nowhere, arrived at a full-out run along the chain, leaping over an obstacle or two like a 100-meter hurdle champion, and dived into the problem car to help the worker sort out the difficulty. In less than five seconds, he came out of the car and reactivated the chain at great speed. Total stop time: 15 seconds. What a show! What efficiency! That said, a North American health and safety supervisor would certainly not approve of how it all happened; in our factories, in any case, that kind of hurry would be condemned—and with good reason in my opinion. But when I asked a Toyota director if the supervisor would be warned not to run like a madman through the factory so as not to injure himself, he didn't understand why the employee shouldn't!

IN JAPAN, REJECTS ARE MEASURED IN PARTS PER MILLION RATHER THAN BY PERCENTAGE

Yes, in Japan, world-class companies measure their rejects in parts per million (ppm). This is an unwritten rule that distinguishes them from other companies.

If you're a Toyota supplier, your contract will stipulate that you have to maintain a reject rate of less than 15 parts per million (ppm) in your factory.

I had the opportunity to tour a Toyota handbrake and door trim supplier. The company had set a goal of less than 10 ppm. By my visit in June 2001, it had reached 2.02 ppm. Mind-boggling! Even better than the 3.4 ppm you can get with the Six Sigma* approach!

Chapter 18

Toyota's Troubles

Between September 2009 and February 2010, the Toyota automobile manufacturing company issued a historic recall of 8.7 million vehicles across the globe, followed by a few other smaller ones. This was one of the most serious crises Toyota had faced in its entire history—a company that had until then built an almost-untarnished reputation.

A HIGHLY PUBLICIZED ACCIDENT

On August 28, 2009, an unfortunate accident involving a rented Lexus (Toyota's luxury brand) caused the death of an American family from San Diego. A conversation between one of the vehicle's passengers and emergency services in the minutes just before the accident was recorded and broadcast widely in the media afterward, giving the public a glimpse of the dramatic nature of the situation.

Many media outlets condemned Toyota straight away, convinced that the accident was due to a defect in the vehicle. It was believed that there had been a sudden unintended acceleration (SUA), or in other words, that the car sped up all by itself. To make things worse, the head of the NHTSA (National Highway Transportation and Safety Administration), Ray LaHood, recommended that Toyota owners stop driving their vehicles[*].

Whipped up by the ensuing media beating, paranoia rose among Toyota owners, and as a precaution, at the request of the NHTSA, the manufacturer issued a number of safety recalls to prevent gas pedals from sticking on some models and other analogous problems. From that point on, complaints from Toyota drivers reporting similar incidents began to pile up.

---

[*] Liker, Jeffrey. *"Toyota's Recall Crisis: What Have We Learned?"* hbr.org, February 11, 2011. [Online] blogs.hbr.org/2011/02/toyotas-recall-crisis-full-of. Accessed February 25, 2014.

It didn't help matters that Toyota was slow to react to the crisis. Competitors had a field day with that, accusing the company of hiding the truth instead of facing the music and explaining themselves to the public. Toyota, they said, had chosen to stick their heads in the sand about even the tiniest problems.

A few months later, called on by the US Congress for a hearing on the crisis, Toyota's CEO, Akio Toyoda, was taken to task repeatedly and felt obliged to apologize both for the slowness of the company's reaction and the assumed vehicle defects.

Personally, knowing the TPS well, my first reaction to the allegations of brake system defects was, "That's impossible!" Nevertheless, I entertained conjectures: "What happened? How could such a major quality problem happen in the factory I toured? How could TPS, which I believed was unassailable, have let such a huge defect go by without it being detected at some point within the manufacturing process?" As a supporter of TPS, I was angry and bitter as I witnessed Toyota being dragged through the mud; but as a consumer, I was disappointed and wondered what on Earth the company's administrators were waiting for to explain things publicly.

*****

The whole story reminded me of a similar problem that I had with a Lexus in 2007. One February night, I wanted to get the car indoors because we were expecting a major snowfall. I started the car and opened the garage door. I only had to move 12 feet to park behind my wife's car. But as soon as I stepped on the gas, the car leaped forward and bang! It smashed into the back of my wife's car, damaging both bumpers. When she heard the noise, my wife ran to see what was happening in the garage. When I explained what had just happened, she looked inside my car and asked if, by any chance, the winter mat, which wasn't perfectly placed, had caught on the gas pedal. I answered that this was the second winter I'd used the mat and I'd never had a problem with it before. I wondered if the wet floor might have caused a slide. Maybe, but one thing was for sure: what had just happened wasn't normal. Panicked, I rushed to the phone and called the Lexus roadside emergency service. I explained my problem to the representative and told him that my vehicle was "possessed." He asked me to bring it in to the dealer to have the problem evaluated. Because I was really scared, I told him I'd never again drive the car. So we agreed that a tow truck would come get the car the next morning.

I spent the night going over every movement, action, and decision that led to me crashing into my wife's car. Had I made a bad maneuver somehow? In a way, I hoped I'd been at fault because I really loved my car!

The next day, I accompanied the tow truck driver to the dealer. I asked the Lexus maintenance service manager, whom I'd always appreciated for his professionalism and friendliness, whether other customers had had the same kind of problem. He assured me he'd never heard a complaint like this one, but for a case this serious, he'd have to send the car's onboard computer report to Toyota in Japan. Three days later, he asked me to come in for a meeting and explained that the Japanese technicians hadn't found anything wrong. The vehicle was in perfect condition. "In perfect condition?" I repeated. "You don't understand! After the traumatizing experience I had, I'm scared to drive this car!" As he leafed through the report, the manager repeated that I had nothing to worry about, because I was driving a Lexus, a car that was and would always be an example of quality and reliability. Last, he added: "Is it possible that your rubber mat caught on the gas pedal?" In the moment, I answered, "Never in a million years!" But I admit that he sowed the seeds of doubt. When I got home, despite my disbelief, I took the time to snip a couple of inches off the width of the mat. And it probably was the cause of the problem, because after that, the incident never happened again.

As my own experience shows, we shouldn't leap to conclusions too quickly. When we're facing a problem, it's better to take the time to investigate and identify the source, as *Kaizen* teaches us! But I can easily imagine that if, in addition to my personal impressions, the press and the country's highest authority in the realm of automobile safety had said so, I too might have thought that Toyota was trying to hide something.

MOUNTAIN OUT OF A MOLEHILL

At the demand of the US Congress, the NHTSA undertook an inquiry into the August 28, 2009, accident. They brought in NASA electronic and software engineers[*] to help them determine whether the Lexus acceleration system could be blamed for the incident and similar ones.

NASA took 10 months to submit its final report. The verdict: no defect that could cause the numerous cases of involuntary acceleration reported by customers was found in the Lexus electronic system[†].

In its report on the accident that led to the crisis, NHTSA showed, clearly and precisely, that the event was due to human error. However, the error wasn't the manufacturer's, but rather the fault of the rental company that had installed a rubber mat that was too wide, not intended for this car model, and that had the effect of catching the gas pedal.

In February 2011, the US Department of Transportation concluded that the reported cases of involuntary acceleration were caused by "poor application"

---

[*] At the time, I didn't understand why NASA was getting involved, but I learned that after the tragic explosion of the *Columbia* space shuttle in 2003, NASA had created the NASA Engineering and Safety Center (NESC), a technical expertise service bringing together more than 400 specialists recruited from all over the world who are called upon to investigate and resolve the most complex problems in every imaginable field of engineering. The center, for instance, helped save the Chilean miners who were trapped in the bottom of their mine in 2010.

[†] NASA. 2011. "NASA's Toyota Study Released by Dept. of Transportation." www.nasa. gov, August 2, 2011. [Online] www.nasa.gov/topics/nasalife/features/nesc-toyota-study.html Accessed February 25, 2013.

of the pedal or by driver error[*]. Toyota's electronic acceleration system was cleared of all blame.

That said, the NASA experts did detect two mechanical problems that needed the manufacturer's attention: a pedal design that made it easy for the pedal to get stuck under the mat, and a pedal that "sticks" and so takes a bit of time to come back to a normal position after being pressed down. Still, this was far from being a SUA.

Did this justify the recall of 8.7 million vehicles and a collective process of such scope? Probably not.

After the fact, some journalists felt that the media's attitude and that of certain American authorities had been inappropriate, and believed they should make amends to Toyota. For example, the prestigious *Bloomberg Businessweek* headline of February 10, 2011, read: "Toyota: The Media Owe You an Apology"[†]. The next day, the venerable *Harvard Business Review* published an article titled "Toyota's Recall Crisis: What Have We Learned?"[‡] The article defended Toyota and condemned the journalists who had launched too quickly into speculation without taking the time to research the topic. The article also blamed the US Congress, which had greatly contributed to dragging Toyota through the mud.

But can we say that Toyota is free of all blame in the affair? Not exactly…

LESSONS LEARNED

The 2009–2010 recall crisis—the worst in its history—threw serious doubt on the Toyota Production System's quality and reliability, although it's clear that the accusations against the company were essentially baseless.

Toyota can still be reproached for its initial silence, followed by rushed public apologies in response to a technical problem that wound up being minor in the end. This approach did them a disservice too. That said, there's quite a difference between Toyota culture and the North American approach. Of course, Toyota's leaders are proud of their system and don't like seeing their reliability called into question. But by the company's philosophy, it's crucial to accept responsibility for one's errors, not to pass the buck to others, and to learn from mistakes.

---

[*] Csere, Csaba. 2011. "It's All Your Fault: The DOT Renders Its Verdict on Toyota's Unintended-Acceleration Scare – The Final Word on the Toyota Unintended-Acceleration Mess." www.caranddriver.com, June 2011. [Online] www.caranddriver.com/features/its-all-your-fault-the-dot-renders-its-verdict-on-toyotas-unintended-acceleration-scare-feature. Accessed February 27, 2013.

[†] Wallace, Ed. 2011. "Toyota: The Media Owe You an Apology." www.businessweek.com, February 10, 2011. [Online] www.businessweek.com/lifestyle/content/feb2011/bw20110210_848076.htm. Accessed February 25, 2014.

[‡] Liker, Jeffrey. "Toyota's Recall Crisis: What Have We Learned?" hbr.org, February 11, 2011. [Online] blogs.hbr.org/2011/02/toyotas-recall-crisis-full-of. Accessed February 25, 2014.

The company can also be chastised for being slow to react in the early hours of the crisis and because its leaders let events get the better of them. But to accuse them of placing profit before customer safety or of trying to hide compromising information is to misunderstand Toyota culture. According to the TPS philosophy, when a problem occurs, it must be examined and studied in depth before coming to conclusions. You first need to go to the *gemba* to see and analyze all possible causes of the reported incidents. That's not a quick process.

In any case, it's true that Toyota failed in its public relations process with customers: when consumers wanted to be reassured and told not to worry, and that the brand's quality and reliability were still worth trusting, the company went silent. I sincerely believe that on this point, Toyota is solely responsible for the mire it found itself in afterward. If Toyota has anything to learn from its American competitors, it's surely in the realm of communication and public relations.

REBUILDING TRUST

Of course, Toyota was cleared in regard to the SUA problem from a technical perspective, but subsequent smaller recalls made it clear that the company no longer has the aura of infallibility we'd been accustomed to. It was inevitable that this would happen one day; as I often say, when it comes to quality management, "zero rejects" remains an objective, even an ideal, even for a company like Toyota that tallies its rejects in parts per million rather than as a percentage. It has generated and will generate defective pieces, nevertheless. There's a low chance that one of them will end up in the car we're driving. Despite everything, Toyota remains an example to follow. Because of the giant mess caused by the media, Toyota had to work overtime to reposition its brand image and win back customers' trust. By all evidence, it's learned from its mistakes—starting in the first quarter of 2012, it had succeeded in recapturing its number-one spot in the world, dethroning the US's General Motors, which had topped it for a time.*

As for me, I never lost faith in Toyota. But I must say, I'm one of the few North Americans who's ever seen TPS in action, and I came out a convert. When you see it, you believe it! I hope that anyone who doesn't get it will take the time to visit one of Toyota's many factories. They'll come out as convinced as I am of the production model's merits!

---

* In a funny turn of events, Toyota's Lexus IS 2014 earned the NHTSA five-star safety rating for all types of collisions!

North American Production Returns to the Fold

The exodus of North American manufacturing (and that of many other so-called "wealthy" countries) to developing countries that offered cheap labor, including China, started in the 1960s and accelerated in the 1980s. But for a few years now, the reverse trend is beginning to pick up steam.

OFFSHORING: A WIN–WIN SITUATION?

Known as offshoring, the phenomenon of transferring production activities to foreign countries covers what some call subcontracting, externalization, or foreign outsourcing. This movement affects all areas of industry, but especially those that require high labor content. So it has especially affected the shoe industry, as well as the textile industry, which now has only a handful of manufacturers in North America. A number of industry heavy-hitters such as Sorel, Brown, Bata, and La Crosse offshored their production to developing countries while smaller players simply couldn't keep up with the wave of Chinese dumping that engulfed us in the early 2000s, and so declared bankruptcy.

Of course, the first reason for a company to offshore its activities to developing countries is to increase the company's profitability, mainly due to cost reduction: the appeal of cheap, abundant labor, inexpensive land, and low-interest loans. In the case of China, there is also a favorable exchange rate due to artificial currency control, government incentives offered to foreign companies, and the opportunity to sell products in China proper, a market that's been greatly expanding for the past few years. For some companies, the fact that their competitors have already offshored their activities, and thus cut their costs, can play into the decision. Other motivations, not always admitted to, may include the opportunity to get away from labor laws or constraining environmental regulations.

Some economists justify offshoring with social arguments: the creation of millions of jobs in poor countries and the resulting increase in quality of life, the fact that job loss in so-called "wealthy" North American and European countries are compensated for to some extent by social safety nets such as employment insurance or income security, the rebalancing of wealth distribution across the planet, and so forth.

Unfortunately, it's not that simple. In reality, in many of these developing countries, human rights are ignored, workplace health and safety standards are nonexistent, and wages are deplorable. And that's not counting the problems of child labor and lack of respect for the environment.

The argument needs nuance. The effects of offshoring are not only positive for the recipient country, and not only negative for the source country.

OFFSHORING ALSO COMES AT A PRICE

When manufacturers say that their main motivation for offshoring their activities is to take advantage of inexpensive labor to reduce their operating costs, I always wonder why they haven't first tried to fix their productivity problems before throwing in the towel. Haven't they heard about the Toyota system, *Kaizen*, or Lean?

In most cases, decision makers, blinded by the idea of savings on labor costs in developing countries, don't take enough time to estimate the overall costs of their supply chains after offshoring, and they neglect to factor into the equation what it might have cost them to make changes to their local production approach. In other words, they're not fully investigating the actual costs of the two scenarios.

Yes, offshoring has a price, and that doesn't just mean adding together the cost price of a product in the developing country of choice with transportation and delivery fees. You also need to include all the "hidden" or indirect costs, such as container warehousing, financing, insurance, and direct customs fees, as well as the salaries of the people who manage all this. If they took all these costs into account, these companies might notice that the difference in cost between local production and offshore production isn't as big as they'd thought. At Genfoot, thanks to over 50 years' experience in the field, we know that the indirect costs for the products we outsource to Asia are around 17%. To make sure we stay competitive, we often compare the cost of our locally manufactured products to what they would have been if we had manufactured them in a developing country. We know that none of these products could have been outsourced to Asia or elsewhere and been delivered here at a lesser cost. And that's not even counting problems with intellectual property, knockoffs, and pollution—virtually guaranteed with outsourcing to Asia—that we're saving.

Another problem with offshore production: productivity and quality are often nowhere to be found. A Grant Thornton study titled "Is China in

TABLE 19.1 Comparison of Average
Hourly Wage for a Chinese Factory Worker
and the Minimum Wage of an American
Worker for the Years 2006 to 2010

Year	China	United States
2006	$0.90	$5.15
2007	$1.12	$5.85
2008	$1.44	$6.55
2009	$1.62	$7.25
2010	$1.84	$7.25

Your Future?"[*] highlights various problems observed in Chinese factories that would be unacceptable in North America:

- A high reject rate: for every million items produced: there's an average of 50,000 defective ones, compared to only 100 in the United States.
- Low efficiency despite the fact that orders are delivered on time: to make up for production delays, they bring in additional workers.
- Lack of worker training and education: this is a serious limiting factor for implementing Lean initiatives and any other productivity improvement method; in fact, only 25% of Chinese factories practice Lean, compared to 70% of American ones.
- Limited use of standardization, continued improvement measures, and stock management methods.

Finally, the report points out that the conditions of Chinese workers are improving (local laws now protect workers' rights better when it comes to overtime, layoffs, and firing), and labor costs are increasing at a higher rate than in North America. That being said, while the average hourly wage for a factory worker more than doubled in China between 2006 and 2010, it only went from $0.90 to $1.84, an increase of $0.94; in this same period, the base minimum wage set by the American government nationwide rose from $5.15 to $7.25, for a total increase of $2.10. Table 19.1 gives a comparison of the average hourly wage for a Chinese factory worker and the minimum wage of an American worker for the years 2006 to 2010.

If we take this further, and compare the average hourly wage—even doubled!—of the Chinese factory worker ($1.84) to that of the American factory worker ($29.75 for 2010[†]), we can see there's no common ground!

---

[*] Grant Thornton LLP. Is China in Your Future? N.d. http://www.grantthornton.com/staticfiles/GTCom/Grant%20Thornton%20Thinking/Resource%20centers/China%20Resource%20Center/China%20Whitepaper%202009%20FINAL.pdf.

[†] Langdon, David and Lehrman, Rebecca (US Department of Commerce – Economics and Statistics) Administration. 2012. "The Benefits of Manufacturing Jobs – Executive Summary." www.esa.doc.gov, May 2012. [Online] http://www.esa.doc.gov/sites/default/files/reports/documents/thebenefitsofmanufacturingjobsfinal5812.pdf. Accessed February 24, 2014.

Still, the situation is evolving in China, and the pace of change could speed up. This is why more and more manufacturers are leaving China to set up shop in Vietnam, Bangladesh, or India, where wages are even lower... until the picture changes there too. As a result, if a company is only looking for the lowest wages as a criterion for moving production to a given country, they have to expect to move production elsewhere every five to ten years!

THE PENDULUM SWINGS BACK

According to a survey for the MIT Forum for Supply Chain Innovation 2012, nearly 34% of American manufacturers surveyed planned to repatriate or reshore their production to the United States[*]. But to do this while remaining competitive in our globalized market, they need a radical change in production philosophy.

This is why many companies that are reshoring production they'd offshored over the past 30 years, such as General Electric (GE), are doing it by implementing Lean initiatives in their factories as well as automation and, above all, innovation. At the Manufacturing's Next Chapter event held in Washington, DC, in February 2013[†], the CEO of GE, Mr. Jeff Immelt, explained how his company's manufacturing had taken up Lean, insisting on the major differences between the way we must produce today and the way we did things 30 years ago. In 2010, GE made a major decision to allot a billion-dollar budget to its manufacturing management team, tasking it to repatriate the manufacturing of water heaters, washing machines, dryers, and refrigerators to the United States over two years. In so doing, they created 1,300 jobs on American soil, in the GE industrial park in Louisville, Kentucky. This billion-dollar sum was invested in changing the culture (a transition toward Lean/*Kaizen*) as well as the procedures and products. One of the most representative examples of this new turn is the new GE water heater, which contains 20% fewer parts and uses 50% less labor.

GE's manufacturing leadership is inspiring; they are true standard-bearers. But we're nevertheless a long way from the 1970s, when the company employed over 23,000 people, compared to only 12,000 today.

I dare to hope that the movement toward reshoring is only beginning, and that we'll see more and more manufacturers get on board with Lean and improve their competitiveness vis-à-vis developing countries.

---

[*] MIT Forum for Supply Chain Innovation and Supply Chain Digest. 2012. "U.S. Re-Shoring: A Turning Point." *MIT Forum for Supply Chain Innovation 2012 Annual Re-Shoring Report.* [Online] mit.edu/events/2012-re-shoring-survey-released-today. Accessed February 22, 2014.

[†] Manufacturing's Next Chapter event held by *The Atlantic* in Washington, DC, February 7, 2013. [Online] events.theatlantic.com/manufacturings-next-chapter/2013. Accessed February 25, 2014.

At Genfoot, we resisted the offshoring trend and decided to invest in Lean and innovation in 1993. As North American companies return to the fold, we're seeing confirmation that we made the right choices, and that our vision of the future at the time had merit despite the circumstances. Today, we continue to reap the benefits of the Lean/*Kaizen* strategy, the path that helped ensure our survival and long-term profitability.

Appendix: Bonus Plans and Productivity Gain-Sharing Plans

SCANLON PLAN

Developed in the 1930s by Joseph Scanlon to save a business from bankruptcy, this plan is based on the following three points:

1. Employee participation
2. Payment of a bonus
3. Employee buy-in to the plan and its objectives

First, employee participation is encouraged by the implementation of a suggestion program and a mixed employer–employee committee. Elected workers meet at least once a month to talk with management about various subjects, such as productivity, cost reduction, quality, and continued improvement. Next, a bonus must reward the employees who contributed to productivity increases. In general, the amount is calculated as follows:

$$\frac{\text{Salaries paid}}{\text{Value of finished products shipped (sales)}} \quad \text{(A.1)}$$

Finally, buy-in to the plan and to the company works through training and debates about objectives, problems, and opportunities. From the stories of companies that have followed this plan, let's remember the following observations:

- Notable productivity increase
- Better teamwork and team spirit
- Better product quality
- Reduced resistance to change
- Increased employee participation and engagement
- Reduced absenteeism

In reality, this plan is more of a management philosophy to improve business performance than it is a bonus program.

RUCKER PLAN

This plan was developed during the Great Depression by Allen W. Rucker, who noted the existence of a direct relationship between the cost of salaries paid and what he called the value of production. He called this relationship "economic productivity." This is a measurement of the value added to the product (output) for each dollar paid in salary (input). This ratio doesn't consider the monetary aspect of production. It doesn't consider quantities; only costs appear. This is the plan's cornerstone. The value added by production is the difference between the revenue generated from sales and the cost of the raw materials consumed for production and delivery.

$$\text{Sales (plus or minus stock variations)} - \text{Cost of raw materials} \quad \text{(A.2)}$$

The measurement of this economic productivity, which appears simple, hides some challenges because it's not always easy to determine the exact cost of the direct or indirect raw materials used.

The plan, which differs somewhat from the Scanlon plan, places the accent on

- Employee participation through a suggestion program
- The creation of various employer–employee committees
- Improvement of communications in general

In this plan, all employees, except those in upper management, receive a percentage of the gains generated. Those who submitted suggestions are officially recognized and rewarded, but not monetarily. Only gains that result from improvements to the basic ratio of salaries paid to the value of production can be shared among employees and management. Companies that have adopted this plan have enjoyed various benefits:

- Optimization of employee motivation
- Improvement in employer–employee relations
- Rapid sales growth
- Increased profitability, among other things, thanks to increased production capacity and improved product quality

IMPROSHARE PLAN

The name Improshare comes from the words "improving," "productivity," and "sharing." The plan, developed in the late 1970s by an American consultant named Mitchell Fein, calculates the gains that result from increased productivity and shares the benefits so generated in equal parts between the employer and the employees. Only productivity gains are shared, and not profits. This plan, relatively recent, is attracting more and more fans because of its simplicity and its easy implementation. Its objective is simple: manufacture more products in fewer work hours—or, more simply, produce more with less.

The productivity ratio, called base productivity factor, or BPF, is obtained by

$$\text{BPF} = \frac{\text{Total real work hours}}{\text{Total standard hours}} \tag{A.3}$$

where the total of real work hours is the sum of all the employees' productive and unproductive time (direct and indirect labor) for a given order, and the total standard hours is the product of the standard time and the number of units produced.

Improshare measures performance rather than dollars saved. It compares the manufacturing times of two successive periods. The value of production hours saved, if applicable, is shared 50–50 between the company and the workers in question, meaning all the production employees who contributed directly or indirectly to the savings.

The advantage of this plan is that it's not at all influenced by variations in sales volume, technological changes, or facility expenses. However, some basic rules are used to make adjustments to the ratio when a new piece of equipment significantly improves production time.

Glossary

5M: Abbreviation of the terms "man, machine, medium, methods, measurements." Method for managing those resources.

5S: Abbreviation of the Japanese terms "*seiri, seiton, seiso, seiketsu, shitsuke.*" The five principles for properly managing a *gemba*: sort, streamline, shine, standardize, sustain. They can be summarized in a single idea: clean and tidy.

***Andon*:** Japanese term meaning "electrical signal light." Signboard with signal lights that, in real time, signals the status of a workstation using lights of various colors. It makes it possible to quickly track down a problem or outage.

Dumping: Practice that consists of selling products in a foreign country at an extremely low price (sometimes lower than local businesses' cost price) in order to liquidate stock or eliminate competition to take over the market. In Canada, dumping is considered a disloyal commercial practice.

Five Whys: Method aiming to determine the source of a problem by questioning the people involved using questions that begin with "why."

***Gemba*:** Japanese term meaning "actual place." Place where the action happens, where the work is carried out. It's the place where added value is created in order to satisfy the customer.

***Gembutsu*:** Japanese term meaning "go and see for yourself." Principle according to which, to be able to understand a problem, one must go to the *gemba* to see it directly, collect all the relevant information (including the supporting documents, rejects, models, tools, etc.), and question the employees who noticed the anomaly. *Gembutsu* is one of the basic elements of the Toyota Production System.

Group technology: Manufacturing technique in which the various machines needed to produce a finished good are grouped together in a module.

ISO 9002: A standard developed by the International Organization for Standardization (ISO) that defines, establishes, and maintains an effective quality assurance system for manufacturing and service industries.

***Jidoka*:** Japanese term meaning "human-supervised automation." Device that makes it possible to stop production as soon as a defective part is produced. *Jidoka* is one of the basic elements of the Toyota Production System.

JIT: See *Just in time.*

Just in time (JIT): Management method that consists of producing only to order, in the quantity requested, a product of superior quality at the best possible cost and delivering it just in time to the customer.

***Kaizen*:** Combination of two Japanese terms meaning "change" and "good," or "change for the better." Concept also known as "continuous improvement," *Kaizen* consists of continually making a multitude of small, low-cost improvements and involving all employees in the process.

***Kanban*:** Japanese term meaning "signboard." Production order card that is always attached to products as they move; it serves as a tool for follow-up and communication.

Lean: Term used by an American researcher from MIT in the late 1980s to simply describe the fundamental ideas of the Toyota Production System's philosophy. Since then, Lean has taken root in the United States and has evolved on its own; while it still largely draws on TPS concepts, American Lean has also developed certain tools that fall outside the strict framework of the TPS.

Manufacturing Resources Planning (MRP): Efficient planning system for all of a manufacturing company's resources. This sophisticated computerized system was developed in the United States in the 1960s and brought to market in the 1970s. While JIT and TQM philosophy was gathering steam in Japan, American managers were learning to use this new production and inventory control system and were working to set it up in their factories. Production using an MRP system is above all job lot production, while JIT is one-piece flow production. The system is also known under the names "Material Requirements Planning" and "Enterprise Resource Planning."

Methods-Time Measurement (MTM): Analysis process for the basic movements that a manual operation requires in order to be carried out (e.g., reach, grasp, move, and position). It assigns each of these movements a predetermined standard time that depends on both the nature of the movement and the conditions under which it is accomplished. It's used in developing standards for short, repetitive cycles.

***Mizusumachi*:** Japanese term meaning "water spider." Handler who supervises the supply of work modules with raw materials, so that these materials are provided to them in small quantities as they are needed.

Modular manufacturing: Pull production process in a factory set up in U-shaped work cells, in which versatile employees work with a one-piece flow approach.

MRP: See *Manufacturing Resources Planning.*

MTM: See *Methods-Time Measurement.*

Muda: Japanese term meaning "waste." Any activity that does not create added value. Seven types of *muda* are present in our companies: those related to overproduction, waiting, transportation, overprocessing, inventory, motion (as in wear and tear on equipment and repetitive strain injuries in people), and defects and rejects. Along with *mura* and *muri*, it is one of the three types of loss, known as 3M, to be eliminated from the *gemba*.

Mura: Japanese term meaning "variability or irregularity in task execution." Along with *muda* and *muri,* it is one of the three types of loss, known as 3M, to be eliminated from the *gemba*.

Muri: Japanese term meaning "unreasonable" or "difficult or exhausting task." Along with *muda* and *mura,* it is one of the three types of loss, known as 3M, to be eliminated from the *gemba*.

OEE: See *Overall Equipment Effectiveness.*

One-piece flow: Production based on each item passing one at a time from one process to the next. (At Genfoot, we called this "hand-to-hand" or "peer-to-peer.")

Overall Equipment Effectiveness (OEE): Ratio that measures the effectiveness of a piece of equipment. It's obtained by multiplying the availability rate by the performance rate and the quality rate: OEE = Availability × Performance × Quality.

Plan, Do, Check, Act (PDCA): Principle for continued improvement and problem-solving tool using the following iterative cycle: you plan the action, carry it out, check the result, and adapt it.

Poka-yoke: Japanese term meaning "anti-error device." System aiming to prevent the production of defective parts.

Pull production: Production that is "pulled" in the sense that a given activity produces only the number of parts used by the next activity. Opposite of push production.

Push production: Production based on forecasts of customer orders or internal needs and not on actual demand. In a push production factory, a given activity may produce as many parts as possible without taking into account the actual needs of the following activity. This operating method leads to the accumulation of in-process stock and finished products. Opposite of pull production.

Productivity gain: Monetary gain resulting from productivity ratio improvement.

QCD: See *Quality, Cost, Delivery.*

Quality, Cost, Delivery (QCD): Performance indicator that relies on three interdependent factors: quality, cost, and delivery. The ultimate goal of *Kaizen* is to produce quality at the best possible cost and in the shortest time.

Quality (Q), Cost (C), and Delivery (D) feedback loop: QCD are all part of the same objective. You cannot cut cost to the detriment of product quality. Likewise, you can't ship defects to make your delivery on time. The feedback loop links these three activities into one and is a key factor in the success of the continuous improvement process.

SDCA: See *Standardize, Do, Check, Act.*

Single-Minute Exchange of Dies (SMED): Quick change method for molds (or dies). It applies to two types of operations: those that are carried out during a machine stop, and those that are done while the machine is working. Its goal is to minimize machine stop-time.

Six Sigma: Improvement approach using statistics that aims to reduce process variations. It results in cost reductions, better execution times, and increased customer satisfaction. The objective is to keep the level of rejects below 3.4 ppm.

SME: Small and medium enterprise.

SMED: See *Single-Minute Exchange of Dies.*

Standardize, Do, Check, Act (SDCA): Cycle that standardizes a procedure. This step is essential before even thinking about undertaking the procedure's improvement.

***Takt*:** From the German term *taktzeit*, meaning "length of cycle." Theoretical length of the cycle to produce an item, adjusted to market demand. *Takt* makes it possible to determine an ideal production pace to avoid both in-process work and delivery delays.

Total Productive Maintenance (TPM): Process aiming to optimize machines' efficiency at all times and prevent outages. It includes several types of maintenance, including autonomous maintenance, preventative maintenance, and reliability maintenance.

Total Quality Management (TQM): Application of quality assurance techniques to all of a company's procedures and processes.

Toyota Production System (TPS): Production system that works with the concepts of just in time and *jidoka.*

TPM: See *Total Productive Maintenance.*

TPS: See *Toyota Production System.*

Traditional manufacturing: Push production process in a factory set up by specialized, procedure-specific departments.

References

Dingus, Victor and William Golomski. 1988. *A Quality Revolution in Manufacturing*. Atlanta, GA: Industrial Engineering and Management Press, Institute of Industrial Engineering, 170 p.

Hall, Robert W. 1983. *Zero Inventories*. Homewood, IL: Dow Jones-Irwin, 329 p.

Imai, Masaaki. 1997. *Gemba Kaizen: A Commonsense, Low-Cost Approach to Management*. New York: McGraw-Hill, 354 p.

Monden, Yasuhiro. 1983. *Toyota Production System: Practical Approach to Production Management*. Norcross, GA: Industrial Engineering and Management Press, Institute of Industrial Engineers, 247 p.

Ohno, Taiichi. 1988. *Toyota Production System: Beyond Large-Scale Production*. Portland, OR: Productivity Press, 143 p.

Osada, Takashi. 1993. *Les 5S: Première pratique de la qualité totale*. Paris: Dunod, 185 p.

Schonberger, Richard J. 1982. *Japanese Manufacturing Techniques: Nine Hidden Lessons in Simplicity*. New York: The Free Press, 260 p.

Sepehri, Mehran. 1986. *Just in Time, Not Just in Japan: Case Studies of American Pioneers in JIT Implementation*. Falls Church, VA: American Production and Inventory Control Society (APICS), 353 p.

Shingo, Shigeo. 1981. *Study of Toyota Production System from Industrial Engineering Viewpoint*. Tokyo: Japan Management Association, 362 p.

Yasuda, Yuzo. 1991. *40 Years, 20 Million Ideas: The Toyota Suggestion System*. Cambridge, MA: Productivity Press, 195 p.

Index